Lives of the Pharaohs

(*overleaf*) Tutankhamun and his wife, Ankhesenamun from an ivory chest found in the Pharaoh's tomb.

Lives of the Pharaohs

Pierre Montet

Member of the French Institute
Honorary Professor at the Collège de France

9/23/74

[signature]

Spring Books

London · New York · Sydney · Toronto

The frieze on pages 5–9 depicts scenes from Egyptian life, as reconstructed by Sir J. Gardner Wilkinson in his book *The Manners and Customs of the Ancient Egyptians*.

This edition published 1974 by
The Hamlyn Publishing Group Limited
London · New York · Sydney · Toronto
Astronaut House, Feltham, Middlesex, England

ISBN 0 600 35452 0

Printed in the Canary Islands by Litografia A. Romero,
S.A., Santa Cruz de Tenerife, Canary Islands (Spain)

Contents

4   A heretic and his successor

5   Greatness and decline

6   A time of conflicts

7   The rule of foreigners

Acknowledgements

Madame T.C. Montet and the publishers wish to thank the following for permission to reproduce the photographs in this book: the Visitors of the Ashmolean Museum, plate 142; Black Star Agency, plates 104, 105, 107, 114 and 193; Ake Borglund (Camera Press), plate 69; Denys Bower, plates 46, 57, 75, 255 and 256; the Trustees of the British Museum, plates 72, 82, 85, 118, 146, 199, 214, 241, 244 and 258; the Directors of the Brooklyn Museum, plate 39; Camera Press, plates 33, 69, 78, 176, 178, 180, 192, 212 and 239; the Syndics of the Fitzwilliam Museum, plates 217 and 238; W. Forman, plate 237; Photographie Giraudon, plates 119, 135, 205, 222, 240, 246, 251 and 257; the Gulbenkian Foundation, plates 63 and 116; Hirmer Verlag, plates 2, 11, 12, 17, 23, 30, 33, 34, 37, 40, 41, 60, 61, 65, 71, 73, 83, 87, 91, 92, 97, 101, 108, 109, 115, 122, 126, 132, 137, 145, 155, 156, 158, 159, 166, 189, 190, 193, 195, 196, 207, 209, 216 and 228; Madame T.C. Montet, plates 191, 226, 227 and 230; Paul Popper, plates 19, 52, 66, 67, 86, 88, 124, 125, 136, 143, 160, 161, 162, 165, 182, 185, 195, 213, 245, 262 and 263; John Pratt (Keystone Press), plate 186; Réunion des Musées Nationaux, plate 233; Umi-Dia-Verlag, plate 265; University College, London, plates 12, 43, 103, 222 and 250, and Roger Wood, plates 20, 25, 26, 27, 28, 45, 46, 47, 48, 51, 58, 76, 93, 94, 111, 112, 129, 130, 147, 148, 169, 173, 174, 175, 201, 202, 219 and 220.

The publishers would particularly like to thank Denys Bower and Roger Wood for all their help in the preparation of this book.

Picture research by Rowena Ross.

1 Builders of the pyramids

Foreword

The Egyptians estimated that there were about three hundred and thirty successive kings on the throne of Horus, from Menes, the founder of dynasty I, to the time of Alexander's conquest.

Most of them are just names on a list. We are fortunate if we can read two tablets about a king, and even more fortunate if we know the length and date of his reign and can attach some fact or event to it: a war perhaps, or the foundation of some building. The artists of the Nile valley were marvellous sculptors, and they carved the effigies of a great number of their sovereigns, in sandstone, granite or limestone; these are priceless records. Unfortunately the Egyptians had little gift for history and narration. Of course there are exceptions, and some of the texts which were composed by Thutmose III, Ramses II and Ramses III deserve to be included in an anthology. I have used these texts extensively, and where they are lacking I have tried to draw words from the stones, and so I have contrived to create a gallery of pharaohs. I hope it will please the reader who knows something about Egypt and would find pleasure, perhaps, in comparing the most original and unusual of the pharaohs with other monarchs of antiquity or the Middle Ages.

Between Menes and the end of dynasty III lay a period of nearly three hundred years, in the course of which a tremendous task was accomplished. Upper and Lower Egypt were united under one authority. The Egyptians evidently went beyond their own frontiers, for we find the name of Khasekhemui, one of the kings of dynasty II, on a fragment of alabaster at Byblos. In Sinai, where turquoise has been worked on since time immemorial, there are many likenesses of the first two kings of dynasty III, Netjrikhe (our Djoser), and Sekhemkhet. The architects had by now given up mud-bricks, and were building temples and tombs of fine limestone. They also erected columns – though, to be honest, these could not yet stand free. The first masterpieces of Egyptian sculpture appeared in the *serdab* of Djoser's mausoleum.

One feels that one would like to make the acquaintance of Djoser, that curious person, with his deeply sunken eyes and prominent cheekbones, but he

Djoser, occupant of the Step Pyramid at Sakkara, the earliest sizeable stone structure built in the world.

is hiding his secrets behind his right hand, which is resting on his breast. He had the distinction of selecting the most remarkable man of his time as his minister: he chose Imhotep, sculptor, architect and physician. In fact Djoser enjoyed all the benefits of his predecessors' work as well as his minister's genius. We have nothing else to say about him.

And now let us begin our gallery of famous pharaohs with a portrait of Snofru, the first king of dynasty IV.

The architects of Sakkara still used decorative motifs, like these columns, that were copied from the old mud buildings.

Imhotep, Djoser's architect, and High Priest of Re at Heliopolis, introduced the pyramid as a fitting tomb for the pharaohs.

Snofru, founder of a dynasty

'And it came to pass that the Majesty of King Huny died and that the Majesty of King Snofru arose as a beneficent king over all the earth.'[1]

So says the author of one of the most ancient books of wisdom to come down to us. According to the lists of kings, Huny was the last king of dynasty III, and Snofru the first, and therefore the founder, of dynasty IV. The Turin Papyrus says that they each reigned for twenty-four years, so presumably Snofru's reign began in about 2620 BC.

The sage whose evidence we have taken does not record whether Huny died a natural or a violent death. He has simply noted a fact. There is no reason to believe that Snofru had been hostile to Huny and his dynasty. But in Egypt, as elsewhere, dynastic changes were sometimes accompanied by bloodshed, and naturally, they also occurred when a king had no male heir.

There are other texts extant which also attribute the virtue of beneficence to Snofru. Must we therefore conclude that Snofru, alone among the pharaohs, left the reputation of a just and merciful man, with a horror of bloodshed? Perhaps we must. At the time of his coronation he added a second name to that which he had been given at birth: he called himself Neb-Maat, Master of Justice, or of Truth. However, unless I am much mistaken, the Egyptians thought a beneficent king was a king who founded cities and built temples, a king who never tired of heaping the votive-tables with offerings, to satisfy the appetites of the gods. And indeed Snofru was a great builder; his mortuary temple contains an incomplete but still ample list of the strongholds and cities he founded.[2] Each foundation is symbolised by a young woman presenting the sign of life and votive offerings, an ewer and two loaves; she also bears on her head, one above the other, the signs of the city and the stronghold. The name of the foundation and, where necessary, the name of the province are engraved alongside. There are four or five foundations in each province. The stronghold is basically a mud-brick enclosure measuring about two hundred by three hundred yards, often more. It contains a temple for the local god, a palace, houses and shops, and since the stronghold was the dwelling of the god and the king, the great religious and administrative dignitaries lived there too. The city is a collection of buildings divided by two streets which intersect at right angles, and ringed by a circular enclosure. All the workers lived in the city, with their livestock.

At the beginning of dynasty IV, the royal titulary had not yet been completely established. It included only a few names. Snofru kept his name of birth as his final name. The three others were coronation names: the name of Horus, the inhabitant of the palace, the name of Nebty (Vulture-Cobra), and the name of Golden Horus.

Since there are gaps in the document, we are unable to determine the total number of Snofru's foundations. For example, the sixteenth nome of Upper Egypt, the nome of the Oryx, had five foundations:

The Joy of Snofru.
The Dances of Snofru.
The Paths of Snofru.
The Nurse of Snofru.
Verdant are the lands of Snofru.

Most of these names did not survive Snofru himself. One of them has been completely changed: 'The Nurse of Snofru' became 'The Nurse of Cheops', while another, Hu-Snofru, has come down through the reigns and centuries to be found in the Late Period as Hesfun.

Each of these strongholds had a temple in which the local god was especially honoured (for Egypt already had as many gods as provinces, or even cities). Certain gods took precedence over others; among them were Ptah of Memphis, Re of Heliopolis, and Hathor, whose temples were everywhere. Snofru was to devote his main effort to the sanctuaries, whose renown stretched beyond the provincial frontiers. The mutilated Annals of the Old Kingdom mention Per-Ur, the Great House, and Per-Nu, the façades of which had masts in front of them, and a golden statue called Horus-Neb-Maat.

If they could, all the pharaohs preferred to live in a palace which they had built themselves, rather than the one their father had lived in. Snofru's palace has disappeared. It must have been in the region of Dahshur, which gave its name to his pyramids, for, according to a very ancient custom which was continued till the end, kings liked to live as near as possible to the site of their mausoleum. Indeed, it may well be that the name Kha-Snofru – meaning 'Snofru appears' – indicated both his temporal and his eternal dwellings: the palace and the pyramid. At the north and south angles of his palace Snofru had two statues erected, one as the king of the South, and the other as king of the North. The doors were made of pinewood imported from Syria.

Snofru was distinguished among the pharaohs for his keen encouragement of ship-building. The difficulty was in obtaining the wood, for Egypt has no forests. Except for the sycamore and the acacia, there was no suitable native timber. All good-quality wood came from northern Syria. Snofru's predecessors, at least since Khasekhemui, the last king of dynasty II, had established relations with the people of Byblos, twenty-five miles north of Beirut, who exploited the nearby forests and, indeed, the forests for miles around. The country of Megau, a dependency of Byblos, also provided the kings of the New Kingdom with pine (*ach*), cedar (*meru*) and juniper (*anu*). We do not know how these relations were established, or how they developed in ancient times. The result is simply recorded to Snofru's credit in a square of the Palermo Stone.[3]

One year, in his shipyards at Memphis, or Bubastis, Snofru built a state ship, of cedarwood, one hundred cubits long, which was called the *Adoration of the Two Lands*. He also built sixty royal barges: these were characterised by the number of transverse beams (there might be as many as sixteen) between port and starboard, which also supported the bridge. Perhaps these royal barges escorted the great ship of state, but they could also have served military and economic purposes, to carry troops or merchandise. The cedarwood or pinewood for this fleet was imported, but the building was done in Egypt. But Snofru also imported actual ships. And here the text presents a difficulty. It reads: 'Import ships forty cubits pine [*ach*].' Does the number forty refer to the ships or the measurements? I think one must take it as forty ships, and assume that they neglected to mention the length. It was in the following year that they built the ship of state – *Adoration of the Two Lands* – in cedarwood, and two ships of state in pinewood.

At the period in question, the horse and cart were still unknown in Egypt. The ship was the only means of 'rapid' transport. Thanks to his fleet, Snofru could reach any point in his kingdom in a few days, and annihilate his enemies. From one expedition to the South he brought back seven thousand prisoners, not to mention oxen and sheep by the thousand; from an expedition in the Tjehnyu region in Libya, he brought back eleven hundred prisoners and again thousands of oxen and sheep. The Egyptians also used ships to transport their engineers, the miners who worked the turquoise beds of Wady Maghara in Sinai, as well as, of course, the troops who ensured security. This working of the turquoise beds must have begun in dynasty II, when the Egyptians first established relations with Byblos.

King Zanakht and King Sekhemkhet had carved fine bas-reliefs on the rocks to affirm Egyptian supremacy. Snofru followed their example.[4] His activity did not pass unnoticed, for texts of dynasties XII and XVIII pay tribute to Snofru the beneficent king.

Among Snofru's successors under dynasty IV, there are at least three whose faces and attitudes are familiar to us, thanks to the wonderful statues in their mortuary temples. When it comes to Snofru we are not so well served. All the same we have two heads in high relief to judge from: one wearing the double crown with uraeus, the other wearing a cap surmounted by two pairs of horns and two feathers. The eyes are wide open, the neck a trifle short. The lips are slightly protruding, and the chin is a little weak. There are two statues which, like the bas-reliefs, come from the mortuary temple near the Rhomboidal Pyramid, but they are very incomplete. The better of the two records an impassive personage with regular features. As far as one can judge, there is no resemblance to Chephren or Mycerinus, but perhaps there is some likeness to Dedefre, Cheops's successor.

Snofru, who founded a dynasty, left no information about his family. He had at least two wives, both of whom survived him. It is possible that Queen

Hetepheres, 'Peace be with her', was a daughter of Huny, for several times in the history of the pharaohs the founder of a new dynasty would marry a daughter of the monarch whom he had supplanted, as if to legitimise his *coup d'état*. Reisner, the archaeologist, found a deeply buried tomb full of magnificent furniture near the pyramid of Cheops; this furniture has been beautifully restored and is now one of the glories of the Cairo Museum.[5] The names of the queen's husband, Snofru, may be read on a canopy, and one can see the names of her son, Cheops, on a chair. It is legitimate to suppose that after her husband's death the queen lived for some time with her son, and that he was concerned with her funeral. There remains one mysterious point. The sarcophagus in the burial-place was empty. The queen's body could not be found. Perhaps it was removed by Cheops himself, but no one knows what became of it.

Snofru's other known wife is called Meritates, 'the Darling of her Father'. She is mentioned on a tablet which reads: 'The royal wife, his beloved, she who is behind the Horus, the ally of the two goddesses [the Vulture and the Cobra]; Meritates, most gracious of Snofru, and most gracious of Cheops, she who was honoured with a pension in the time of Chephren.' Meritates married Snofru when she was very young. It has even been claimed that she was his daughter. She was still young and beautiful on the death of Snofru. She delighted his successor, Cheops, but passed unrecorded through the reign of Dedefre and died in the time of Chephren. Her tomb has not been found.

Snofru had numerous sons. The only one of historical interest is his successor Cheops. Among the important personages of his reign, two are quite well known: Rahotep and Meten. From Rahotep's tomb at Meidum come the companion statues, virtually intact, of the master of the tomb and his wife, Nufrit the beautiful. As a legitimate royal son, Rahotep was well provided with religious and civil titles: chief of transports, keeper of quivers, chief of soldiers. And yet I have never looked at this statue without being struck by its expression of fear. The cudgel was an excellent means of government in ancient Egypt, which sometimes fell even on the shoulders of the great. Was Rahotep afraid of some disgrace or of marital misfortunes? Nufrit, chastely enveloped in her cloak, is quite a fine woman, rather fat, with a slightly receding chin, a woman who, one feels, could not have had any great anxieties.

Meten's tomb is now in the Berlin Museum. He was the guardian of numerous strongholds and the administrator of several nomes, most of them in the Delta. He had inherited some servants and flocks from his father, together with an estate of fifty arouras (about thirty acres) from his mother, but he managed to increase this inheritance: he acquired a further two hundred arouras on condition that he provided a hundred loaves a day for a dead queen (perhaps it was the king's mother, Ni-Maat-Hep). On the king's death he became guardian of Snofru's mortuary temple, and by the end of his

Statues, like these of Prince Rahotep and his wife Nufrit, were put in tombs as residences for the spirit if the actual body was destroyed.

life he possessed a fine estate with fruit-trees, a lake and a vine.

The inscriptions of such personages and their contemporaries give us an impression of tranquillity and comfort. The public peace was not disturbed and a good employee could easily make sure of his daily bread for his old age, together with his posthumous prosperity.

A king cannot only be concerned with affairs of state: he has the right to enjoy himself. One day, however, Snofru found himself idle, and bored with everything. (A bored king is a popular theme in many literatures – perhaps there really is such a thing. The monarch of ancient times was surrounded by courtiers who attempted to satisfy his desires before he had even expressed them, and he suffered more from boredom than the poor beggar who was worried about tomorrow.) Snofru did not know what to do. He summoned his chief of ceremonies, who suggested something which might please his master.[6] Why did Snofru not 'man' a barge with the most beautiful women in his palace? – 'You will see them row, and you will see the river banks, the fields and the bushes.' The king called for twenty oars of ebony and gold and twenty pretty girls who had not lost their figures through maternity, twenty girls with perfect breasts. He did not order them to undress. He was more subtle, he commanded them to wear net to swathe their charms in mystery. Contemplating them as they rowed, he found that he was happy. But the leading girl, who was fiddling with her tresses, dropped her turquoise fish into the water. She stopped, and the whole crew stopped rowing. 'Why have you stopped?' asked Snofru. When she told him he offered to replace the jewel, but the girl preferred the one she had lost. The king did not know what to say. However, the master of ceremonies, a magician, was not to be troubled by so trivial a problem. He placed one half of the water on top of the other and so presented the girl with her little fish.

Another day, Snofru had just dismissed his counsellors but had second thoughts and called them back again. They prostrated themselves before him, and he announced his desire: – 'Let someone go and find the king a man of wit, an eloquent speaker.' The counsellors thought of a master of ceremonies of the goddess Bastet, who was a skilful scribe and a wealthy man.[7] He was presented, and the king said: 'Speak fine words to me, and choice speeches which My Majesty will be pleased to hear.' But he did not simply want intellectual satisfaction. He was anxious about the future, and he recorded on papyrus what the sage revealed to him.

All this belongs to popular literature, but we have no reason to disbelieve these two stories except, perhaps, the magician's intervention. Mehemet-Ali liked to dally in his marble pool at Shubra while the women of his harem bathed in their veils. Other pharaohs besides Snofru wanted to know the future and were not ashamed to consult prophets.

The pyramids of Snofru

As we know from the behaviour of certain other pharaohs, a king did not wait until he was old before he thought about his mausoleum. The burial-place was often the most important business of the reign. This was certainly the case with Snofru, who had founded a city, called the City of the Two Pyramids, on the edge of the desert near the modern village of Dahshur. A causeway led from the City of the Two Pyramids to Snofru's own pyramid, not as huge as the great pyramid of Cheops, but still a mighty monument, about three hundred feet high. The burial-chamber had a corbelled roof (which seems to have been popular in Snofru's time) and the neighbouring tombs date from his reign. Some distance away, one's attention is caught by one of the most remarkable monuments of the Libyan plateau, the Rhomboidal Pyramid, so-called because the gradient of each face has been changed half-way up. There can be no doubt that this pyramid belonged to Snofru. His name has been found on blocks, and we can read it time and time again in the mortuary temple. The most astonishing thing is that this pyramid had two entrances, two passages and two chambers, both with corbelled roofs. The effect is

The Rhomboidal Pyramid that Snofru built at Dahshur is unusual not only in its shape, but because it had two entrances and burial chambers.

awe-inspiring. The explanation for this is probably very simple. While the burial-chamber was being built, someone noticed that it was not perfect. It was reinforced with cedar beams, and finally they decided to build a new chamber; but it is not known where the king was actually buried.

Two pyramids for a single king is already enough. Three, surely, is too many.[8] However, there is a third pyramid attributed to Snofru, and this is the pyramid of Meidum. Those who attribute it to him are not modern scholars, but scribes who visited the site at the time of the Middle Kingdom and traced graffiti on the walls of the burial temple. They certified that the monument was in perfect condition, and that it belonged to Snofru. (The neighbouring tombs are, moreover, those of functionaries who lived at the beginning of dynasty IV.) There was no trace of the personage who was buried in the pyramid, any more than there had been at Dahshur. But we are not completely at a loss. The Meidum pyramid was originally a step pyramid like the Djoser pyramid at Sakkara. This type of pyramid was in use throughout dynasty III. It was turned into a perfect pyramid by the addition of a coat of limestone, so that we may see it as marking the transition between two

The Step Pyramid, built by Imhotep at Sakkara for the pharaoh Djoser. Imhotep was one of the first to use limestone blocks for building.

dynasties. It is now generally accepted that this pyramid was begun at the end of dynasty III for its last sovereign, Huny, and that it was altered by Snofru. It is possible that as the founder of a new dynasty Snofru thought of appropriating his predecessor's work; and then, perhaps, he changed his mind, fearing a posthumous vengeance from the king who had been dethroned and despoiled. Then he had the idea of building a funerary monument near Dahshur, not far from the palace where he lived, which had the same name: Kha-Snofru. At Meidum, Snofru's memory has cast Huny's into the shade.

In spite of precautions to make Snofru's work respected and to assure him of his funerary cult, all sorts of people, even officials, did just as they liked with the personnel and appurtenances of the two pyramids. Stone-robbers removed the stones from the causeway up to the monuments and even requisitioned the personnel and the livestock.

To Pepi I, of dynasty VI, such abuses seemed intolerable. Snofru was wise to have left a reputation for beneficence. No doubt it was this reputation which led Pepi to ensure that the pyramids, the city and its inhabitants were respected.

Cheops, the Great Pyramid and the Sphinx

Cheops, the son of Snofru and Queen Hetepheres, was born in a city of the sixteenth nome of Upper Egypt, the nome of the Oryx where his father had been born before him. It was then called 'the nurse of Snofru'. After the birth of Cheops it became Menat-Khufwey, 'the nurse of Cheops', and this name became permanent.

The principal god of the region was Chnum, the ram god. And so the royal child was called Chnum-Khufwey, 'Chnum is his protector'. Even in contemporary texts, the name was often shortened to Khufwey, which the Greeks transcribed as Cheops. On his coronation, Cheops added three new names to this princely title. His Horus name was Medjdu, 'he who commands'; his Vulture-Cobra name was Medjd-r-Nebty, 'he who commands for the two goddesses'. As his Golden Horus name, he chose Horuy, the Horian. These names were not selected at random, they foretold the tendencies of the reign. Cheops did great things and was a demanding and authoritarian master.

Herodotus maintains that Cheops reigned for fifty years, and Manetho even says that he reigned for sixty. The scholars of the Late Period, and the Greeks, assumed that whoever built a monument like the Great Pyramid must have reigned a long time. However, the Turin Papyrus, which is generally well informed, reduces the length of the reign to twenty-three years, and we will keep to this figure.

Wonderful statues of Dedefre, Chephren and Mycerinus, the successors of Cheops, have been found in their mortuary temples, but nothing comparable remains in the mortuary temple of Cheops, which was levelled to its foundations. We must content ourselves with an ivory statuette of somewhat mediocre workmanship. It seems that the sons and successors of Cheops bore no resemblance to him. Cheops had a rather heavy face, with a somewhat prominent jaw.

Meritates, Snofru's wife, was certainly one of Cheops's wives. She survived him, and even survived his successor Dedefre. She lived for some time with Chephren, who was concerned with her mausoleum, just as Cheops had been concerned with the burial-place of his mother Hetepheres. The names of the nine sons and daughters of Cheops have been found in the texts. Among them we should remember those of Dedefre and Chephren, who succeeded him. We should also note those of Dedephor, who presented him with a prophet and magician, and Princess Henutsen, of whom we shall speak later.

According to a late inscription, Cheops founded the temple of Hathor at Dendera. Hathor was the great goddess who guided the navigators, and Cheops had good reason for showing piety to her. The names of Cheops have been found on granite pillars at Bubastis and Tanis. These two cities could be ports of call for fleets which came down the Mediterranean to Byblos and down the Red Sea to the Terraces of Turquoise. At Sinai, not far from the reliefs already mentioned, there is a bas-relief of Cheops vanquishing a Mentu barbarian. In the goddess's temple at Byblos, Cheops's envoys left some alabaster vases engraved with his name and that of Queen Meritates. Some of the founders of the temple of Ptah, who lived under Cheops and his successors, have engraved their names and titles in the valley of Rohanu, a few days' march from Coptos.[1] It was a favoured place, where they could find a good well, gold, and blocks of stone from the mountain, which they only had to slide down to the road and drag as far as Coptos.

All the granite which was used by Egyptian architects and sculptors came from the Aswan region. The Aswan quarries were already being exploited in the days of Cheops. The prospectors, who were constantly crossing the southern deserts, found a bed of diorite: a stone which was even harder and finer than granite. For a long time archaeologists looked for this bed in vain; it was discovered by frontier guards in 1938, forty miles or so from Abu Simbel.[2] A stela engraved with the words 'the quarry of Cheops' was found at the top of a mound. Even reaching this diorite bed was an achievement in itself, for the desert is more barren here than anywhere else. Once they had left their departure base and provisions centre near Abu Simbel, the men who were to work in the quarry were forced to depend on the water in their leather bottles. The journey back, with their burden of stones, was even more

This is the only known representation of Cheops, builder of the Great Pyramid at Giza.

arduous than the journey out. The diorite bed was exploited during the Old and Middle Kingdoms, and then abandoned.

While Cheops was making the most of the country round about, he was also receiving visitors from afar, the Helu-Nebut for example, who might be considered the ancestors of the Hellenes. We have unexpected information about this from a bas-relief which almost certainly comes from Cheops's mortuary temple,[3] on which three majestic oxen are named:

'Cheops is lapis-lazuli.'

'[That which] the Helu-Nebut [ships] cross belongs to the Golden Horus Horuy.'

'The herald of the Helu of the lands belongs to Cheops.'

Like the names of provinces, of which there were so many in the Old Kingdom, these names are composed of a phrase made up of a subject and an attribute. The Egyptians adored giving names to all sorts of things, such as animals – horses, when they had them, or dogs and cows.

I suppose the three oxen simply received the name of the province to which they belonged. The attribute for the first one is the name of the region where the Egyptians procured their much-used lapis-lazuli; the name of this particular stone is the adjective for blue. One can choose between three translations: Cheops is an inhabitant of the Tefrer; Cheops is lapis-lazuli; Cheops is blue. In the second and third names the Helu seem to be divided into two branches: the Helu of the ships and the Helu of the lands. 'That which the Helu cross' is a way of describing the Mediterranean, which Cheops already claimed as his own. The Helu of the lands were those who were trying to settle on Egyptian territory; an interpreter was necessary to establish relations with them. It is possible to form some idea of these Helu. From the most ancient times, as in the times of the Saite kings, they were sailors, pirates and traders. It was the north wind which pushed them to the shores of Egypt. They were not averse to making a sudden attack, but if they were allowed to set foot anywhere, they soon settled there for good. Cheops's text is the first record of their presence in Egypt.

The kings of the Old Kingdom soon got into the habit of going up the Nile as far as the residence of Elephantine, coming down it in short stages and stopping to found or to beautify sanctuaries. There is no doubt that Cheops did this, but we have no reason to believe that he himself led the expeditions which he sent into Sinai, to the valley of Rohanu, to Byblos and to Nubia, and, with better reason, into Mesopotamia and the country of the Helu. Leading expeditions was the task of the heads of missions, who transmitted orders to the local dignitaries – orders which were always carried out, and reported back to the king. Without even leaving his palace, Cheops reigned over a territory which was much vaster than Egypt itself. He learned from the experience of the pharaohs of dynasty III and those of his father Snofru; and, almost without bloodshed, he managed to give his kingdom a power

(*opposite*) Furniture of dynasty IV from the tomb of Hetepheres, wife of King Snofru. The wooden parts are modern restorations, the gold and silver are ancient.
(*overleaf left*) Head of Nufrit from a statue found in her tomb at Giza.
(*overleaf right*) Seneb, Chief Dwarf of the Royal Clothing, seated with his wife.

unequalled during the Old Kingdom and which would only just be equalled by the most famous sovereigns of dynasty XII. In the New Kingdom, Thutmose III would carry Egyptian power even further, but only through a great military effort.

It was the knowledge of his power which inspired Cheops with the desire to raise the Great Pyramid of Giza as his tomb. It was a pyramid far greater than those of Meidum and Dahshur. Cheops' successor, Chephren, would almost equal it, but other kings would not even try to rival him.

The Great Pyramid, which the ancients listed among the wonders of the world, has so often been described and illustrated that I need only insist on a few points here. The pyramid is the tomb of the king, but it is also much more than this. It is a deity, the king himself; not the mortal personage who for some years sat on the throne of Horus, but a being whose destiny it was to be immortal. This is why all the pharaohs gave their pyramid a title composed of their own name and an attribute. The name that Cheops chose, Khufwey-Akhety, is significant. It means 'Cheops is an inhabitant of the Akhet', that is, of that region of the world where the rising sun appears at points which vary slightly throughout the year. The east face of the pyramid is therefore the most important. It is towards the east face that the rising causeway turns when it leaves the temple of the valley to reach the temple of the cult. Boat-shaped excavations have been made in the rock on the right and left of the causeway there, to facilitate the mooring of Cheops's two solar boats (the *mandjit* for the day, the *mesketet* for the night), when they moor close to the pyramid to collect or return their royal passenger. There was a vignette made in the days of the New Kingdom for King Teti of dynasty VI, but nothing prevents us from applying it to Cheops; it shows the inhabitant of the pyramid, not stretched out in his sarcophagus, but erect inside the monument as if he was supervising the movements of the boats.

Cheops's architects managed to orientate the pyramid, and especially the eastern face, with extraordinary precision (the deviation is less than two and a half minutes). No observation of the sunrise, or measurements taken from the Nile, could have given them such accuracy. No doubt they corrected their calculations by means of astronomical observations, but modern scholars have failed to agree on the method they used. This precision was intended to facilitate the journey of the two solar boats and therefore the whole posthumous life of the king.

In 1954 a completely unexpected discovery was made near the south face of the pyramid. The Service des Antiquités had decided to strip the accumulated rubbish from the lower layers of the monument, not for scientific reasons, but to help the tourists get round more easily. During this clearance, two structures were discovered: they were set end to end, long and low, and covered with thick slabs of limestone. So far only one of these structures has been examined. The blocks from the roof were lifted off and put to one side.

The large pyramid of Chephren and the smaller one of Menkare, built at Giza during dynasty IV.

The pyramids at Giza seen across the desert.

Some of these blocks bore graffiti in red ink, and one could read the name of Dedefre, Cheops's son and successor, who was concerned with his father's burial. Egyptologists had been unable to agree on the order of succession of the kings of dynasty IV, and this information was therefore welcome. But what were much more important were the contents of the structure: inside was found a big cedarwood barge which had been dismantled and then reconstructed. Someone had evidently been content to put the planks in position without fixing them together again, but for some years now we have been able to see the completely reconstructed barge. Unfortunately the shed which now contains it is too small, and this has prevented the adjustment of the prow, which is shaped like the umbel of a papyrus. This masterpiece of boat-building, the *Adoration*, belongs to that series of state barges of a hundred cubits, called *Illumination of the Two Lands*, launched by Snofru. A graceful wooden canopy on the bridge sheltered the king as he steered.

Where did he steer to? Perhaps we shall know when the second excavation has revealed its contents. One suspects that it contains a second barge. Might these not be the *mandjit* and the *mesketet*? If they are, then the first barge would have been equipped with the many accessories which were considered essential for solar boats. The fact that the barge possessed few oars seems to indicate that a towing barge was needed. If the second barge is well equipped with oars, we shall be dealing with two different types of boats, a towing and a travellers' barge, the kind that one so often sees on figurative monuments. If this theory is correct, the king expected to visit the most venerable places of pilgrimage, like Abydos, Busiris, Mendes or Buto. We must contain our speculation on this point until the second excavation is explored.

Almost exactly halfway between the pyramids of Cheops and Chephren there is another monument which has attracted the attention of travellers since antiquity. This is the Sphinx. Egyptologists have debated the question of its date and for a long time they saw it, without the slightest proof, as a work of the Middle Kingdom. The modern tendency is to attribute it to Chephren, since the causeway which goes up to the second pyramid passes close to the monster. But could we not argue that this route was taken to avoid the Sphinx, and therefore that the Sphinx already existed?

All the Egyptian texts describe the Sphinx as Harmachis, Har-em-akhet, 'Horus in the horizon'. One must remember that Cheops called himself an Akhety, an inhabitant of the Akhet, a subject of the rising sun. When he had taken possession of the plain of Giza to build his funerary monument, he could have been the first to notice this rock. It had the form of a lion *couchant* turned towards the rising sun and he ordered his sculptors to complete the work begun by nature.

Labourers of Asiatic origin, working in the region in dynasty XVIII, thought they recognised the Sphinx as Hurun, a god of their own country. The

(*opposite above*) A queen did not have the position and dignity of the pharaoh, and so was buried in a smaller pyramid, like these three at Giza.
(*opposite below*) View from the summit of Cheops's pyramid over the ancient burial ground for nobles and members of the royal family.

The Great Pyramid and the Sphinx, which probably originally bore the features of Cheops. Its Arabic name means 'the father of fear'.

Sphinx is also mentioned under the name of Hurun-Harmachis on a monument which was found near a small pyramid nearby; this pyramid was known as the stele of the daughter of Cheops. On this stele one can in fact read the titles of Cheops and the name of one of his daughters, Princess Henutsen; no one dates the stele as early as dynasty IV. No doubt it is a copy done from the original during dynasty XXI. This record also associates several monuments of which traces still exist: a temple of Isis, a temple of Osiris, the princess's pyramid and the temple of Hurun-Harmachis. This last must not be confused with the granite temple, which is often mistakenly known as the temple of the Sphinx, but which is in fact the reception temple of Chephren.

Of course we do not have the actual decree in which Cheops ordered the sculpting of the Sphinx. That would be expecting too much. Let us simply note that the topographical and epigraphical indications strongly associate the Sphinx, the image of Harmachis and King Cheops-Akhety.

And so it was that two of the greatest and most famous monuments of Egypt, the Great Pyramid and the Sphinx, were executed in the reign of Cheops, according to his orders and plans. They bear witness to the extraordinary power which the pharaoh had managed to acquire.

Cheops did not leave a very good reputation among the Egyptians. Herodotus records that he heard in the streets of Memphis that Cheops's finances had been exhausted by his extravagant expenditure on the buildings; that he had been forced to close the temples and had even ordered his daughter to do what she could to procure funds. The first at least of these statements might be correct. [4]

Cheops believed himself to be an inhabitant of the Akhet, a being nearer the gods than humankind; he considered, quite naturally, that the mass of his people ought to work for a good twenty years at his funerary monument. He felt no remorse at sending his best workmen and legions of labourers into the inhospitable desert to extract the granite, the diorite and the gold, the turquoise and precious stones. Everyone in Egypt who was not working in the fields toiled in the service of the king, without the slightest complaint. Cheops certainly deserved the name he had given himself: Medjdu, 'He who commands'.

As in the case of other despots, this ruthlessness was accompanied by exemplary courtesy. This aspect of Cheops's character comes to light in the Westcar Papyrus, famous in Egyptology. On it is told how Cheops assembled his sons in his palace; each one told him a story about a magician, and Cheops thanked him by giving a fine offering to the magician and to the son who had witnessed the miracle. Dedefre was the last to speak. He told his father about an old man of a hundred and ten who knew a vast number of spells, and knew the number of secret chambers in the sanctuaries of Thot, which Cheops greatly wanted to find and use. By river and road Dedefre made his way to the old man, greeted him with a fine compliment, and bade him return to

Cheops's court. 'How is it', asked Cheops, 'that I have not seen you until now?' – 'He who has been called comes to you. They have called me, I have come.' The old man performed a few spells, and then revealed to Cheops that the wife of a priest of Re was pregnant with three children, who were to have a beneficent influence over the whole earth. At this news the heart of His Majesty fell into sadness, but the magician cheered him: the three children would not reign for some time yet. Cheops, however, still hoped that he would manage to be in the right place at the right time to prevent the fulfilment of this prophecy. If we knew the end of the story we should probably learn that all Cheops's efforts were to prove useless – for as more than one sage has observed, 'Man proposes, God disposes'.

Pepi II, a centenarian king

The reign of Mycerinus, grandson of Cheops, and builder of the third pyramid, was followed by three or four others about which we know almost nothing. Then came the kings whom the ancient prophet had predicted to Cheops. They owed their origin to the god Re himself and to the wife of a priest of Re, lord of Sakhebu, a city which actually existed in the nome of the Cuisse, north-west of Memphis. At Abusir, between Giza and Sakkara, three of these kings built pyramids which form a small copy of the group at Giza. These kings were the first to build the solar temples, with their open courtyard and short, stumpy obelisk in the middle. During this period the art of bas-relief reached a perfection which it was not to know again until the time of Amenhotep III. The tombs of Tjey and of Ptah-hotep at Sakkara, discovered in the middle of the last century, are among the most striking monuments of Egyptian art.

Unis, who is thought to be the last king of dynasty v, was an enterprising sovereign in the maritime and colonial spheres. He was also the first to introduce copies of texts in the inner chambers of his pyramid: they were copies of the texts which Cheops would have liked to procure for his own mausoleum. King Teti, who succeeded him, apparently did not belong to his family. He had married Queen Iput, who had a rather curious title, for she was the Royal Mother of the Pep-Men-Nofer Pyramid. Thenceforward, the royal women always added the name of the reigning sovereign's pyramid to their own title. The dead king was completely identified with his pyramid – it was one with the king who inhabited it.

Tjey was Curator of Monuments during dynasty v and his large mastaba-chapel at Sakkara suggests this was an important position.

Pepi I, who succeeded Teti, had two wives, who both bore the title of Royal Mother of the Pyramid of Meryre. It was the second, Ankhnaspiopi, who gave birth to Neferkare Piopi, our Pepi II. The Brooklyn Museum has a rather pretty statuette which represents Pepi II on his mother's lap. She is sitting on a low-backed chair, and the young king is resting his feet on a seat which forms a right angle to it. His figure and attitude are those of a child, but his face is that of an adult. Perhaps, as a critic has suggested, the statue is a work of propaganda meant to affirm the queen's authority during the king's childhood. The work also has the merit of being intact.

According to Manetho, Pepi II was only six years old when he succeeded Meryre, and he was over a hundred when he died. The first point is confirmed by a letter which the young king wrote at the age of nine. There is an obviously childish style about this letter, which I shall quote in its entirety later on. The second point is supported by the Turin Papyrus and by a passage in a famous text, *The Admonitions of an Egyptian Sage*, which alludes to the extreme old age of the reigning king.

Pepi II is known to have had three wives: Queen Neith, the daughter of Pepi I, Queen Iput and Queen Udjebten. All three bore the title 'Royal Woman of the Pyramid of Neferkare-Men-ankh'.

The young king's first act was to send a letter (which he sealed himself) to a man of Aswan, called Harkhuf, who had three times explored the land of Yam: this was an ill-defined region between the First and Second Cataracts, inhabited by people who were somewhat hostile to their neighbours. On his third voyage Harkhuf had obtained ample supplies of ebony and ivory, panther skins and living animals, but he had also had the good fortune to find something infinitely more rare, a dwarf who danced like a god. Dwarfs were reputed to be good dancers, but this one had exceptional worth; to find his like one normally had to go to the Punt country (this had been done, more than half a century earlier, under King Izozi, by a man called Bawerded). When he received the explorer's report, only one thing mattered to the young sovereign; it was absolutely essential that the dwarf should be brought back to his court, 'alive, well and healthy'. Here, then, is what Pepi wrote, or rather what he dictated:[1]

The King himself has sealed, in the year of the second time [of taking a census of the flocks, that is to say the year 3], the third month of the flood, the 15th.
By Royal Command, to the unique friend, master of ceremonies, chief interpreter Harkhuf:
I know the contents of your letter which you have written for the presence of the King, for the archives [Harkhuf was not distinguished enough to write directly to the king, but his report had been read in high places]; in this letter you tell me that you are going down in peace from the land of Yam with the soldiers who were with you. In this letter you say you are bringing back all the great and beautiful things which Hathor, the lady of Imau [a city in the nome of Occident, north-west of Memphis,

Statuette of Ankhnaspiopi, Pepi I's wife, with her son, the future Pepi II.

where Hathor had a sanctuary] gave to King Neferkare, may he live everywhere and for ever. You said in your letter that you were bringing back a dwarf [*deng*] who dances like the god of the land of the Akhetiu. [Akhet is the land of the rising sun and the Akhetiu are its real or imaginary inhabitants.] You have said in the presence of My Majesty that there was never a man who had travelled to the land of Yam who had brought back his like. Have you not said that you would do what was wanted, what was praised by your master, that whether you were watching or sleeping in my service you would do what your master wants and praises?

My Majesty will make your fortune in quality and in quantity for the benefit of your son's son through all generations, so that all men who learn what My Majesty has done for you will say: 'There is nothing to be compared with what has been done for the unique friend Harkhuf, when he went down into the land of Yam, because of the vigilance which he exercised in doing what was wanted, what was praised, and what was commanded by his master.'

(*left*) Model of a scribe, dynasty v. (*opposite*) A dynasty v tomb model of a servant girl grinding corn.

After the generalities, Pepi II comes down to concrete things:

Come, then, when you come down the Nile, come straight to my palace. Make haste. Bring me this dwarf whom you are bringing back from the land of the Akhetiu; bring him back alive, well and healthy [these three adjectives are part of a well-known formula] to dance like a god, to rejoice and delight King Neferkare. When he comes down the Nile with you, put vigilant men around him on both sides of the boat. Take care that he does not fall into the water. When he sleeps at night, send guards to sleep round him in his cabin, which guards must be changed ten times a night [sentinels were no doubt relieved every hour by the head of the section]. My Majesty wants to see this dwarf more than the marvellous products of Punt. If you reach the palace and this dwarf is with you, alive, well and healthy, My Majesty will do great things for you, more than was done for the divine sealer Bawerded in the time of Izozi, according to the delight which My Majesty will feel to see this dwarf.

Orders have been sent to the chiefs of the new cities, to the unique friends and the prophets to tell them to take their victuals into all the administration's strongholds and all the temples. There is no exception to this rule.

(These last words were not unnecessary; the Egyptian state was growing poor by exempting most of the temples from rules which the king himself had decreed.)

During his reign, Neferkare Piopi must certainly have had other occasions to welcome dwarfs who 'danced like gods', for the Egyptians and the people of Byblos had together established a navigation route which went from Byblos to Punt, from the Seaports of Pine to the Seaports of Incense. This fact emerges from a brief inscription engraved on a tomb at Aswan which dates from Pepi II. 'The majordomo Chnum-hotep says: I have gone with my masters the princes and sealers of the god Teti and Khuye to Byblos and to Punt, eleven times I have gone to these lands.' The record of this humble navigator is valuable, establishing as it does that his ship touched Byblos and

Punt eleven times. One can therefore safely assume that the *kebenit*, with mixed Egyptian and Syrian crews, left Byblos, followed the Mediterranean coast as far as the first navigable tributary of the Nile, the Avaris tributary, entered the Bitter Lakes by way of the Tumilat Wady, reached the Red Sea and followed the African coast as far as Punt, where they knew that they were expected.[2]

Such voyages were not without risks. Even under Pepi II, Egyptian sailors were on one occasion attacked and massacred by nomad Arabs while they were busy caulking their *kebenit*, to set sail to Punt. This unfortunate incident took place at the Mountain of the Aamu and there has been much discussion about the site of this mountain, which I think I can place in the Lebanon. Byblos was a city inhabited by Aamu, and among these people the Egyptians had as many enemies as friends. When King Neferkare was told of the massacre, he ordered an enterprising man of Aswan to bring back the bodies of these Egyptians who had died for their country.

The king had ended his letter to Harkhuf with the imperative words, addressed to all those whom Harkhuf might have to have recourse to for victuals as he came down the Nile: 'There is no exception to this rule.' He was aware, and his counsellors were certainly aware, that most of the temples considered themselves excused from contributing to the state expenses, justifying their claim by some ancient decree. We have an abundant collection of these decrees of immunity, which seem to have multiplied under dynasty VI, and Pepi II was no less guilty than his predecessors. There are many other examples, but we will choose a decree made by Horus Netjerkhau (Pepi II), in the year after the Eleventh Time (the year 22). This was addressed to the Director of the Domain of the Pyramid, the Judge of the Gate, the Vizier, the Director of the South, to Dja'u, the Director of the Royal Scriptures, to Huy, the Commander of the South, to the Director of the Prophets, to the Inspector of Prophets and to all the labourers who brought in the harvests of the temple of Min, to the functionaries and companions of Min, the watchers, and the agents of the shops of this temple.

My Majesty does not allow the aforementioned people to be enlisted in the royal service, because they are reserved for Min of Coptos. The high functionaries named in the premises of the decree will be revoked if they disobey this order.

The decree ends with a curious commentary:

As for the things which are said about My Majesty [evidently gossip]: that there exist sealed orders from the king to raise labour for the king's works in the south . . . and also that this order makes no exception whatever in the reserved domains in the south, My Majesty does not allow any people whatever in the temple of Min to make any deliveries or collections, or any contribution to any of the works which are done in the south. King Neferkare living for ever for eternity has reserved them for Min of Coptos for all eternity.[3]

Relief from the temple of Min at Coptos. Min embodied the abstract male principle and was worshipped until Roman times.

If Harkhuf had called for help as he passed the temple of Min of Coptos with his boat and his precious passenger, the attendants would almost certainly have shut the door in his face; unless, that is, Harkhuf had been accompanied by people who were not disposed to accept refusal. In fact things had developed into a desperate struggle between the royal officials, who had to work and carry out their orders, and the priests of Min and of other gods who rested on their privileges and did not want to lose them. In other words, by multiplying exceptions throughout the length and breadth of the land, the pharaohs until Pepi II had simply organised anarchy. Every order clashed with a counter-order. The strongest or the most cunning survived, and things went on as best they could.

Pepi II seems not to have had very good morals, if we are to believe a popular tale which was published some years ago. This tale reveals that the king indulged in practices which were condemned by religion and particularly condemned in the nome of Memphis where he was living. Late at night, Pepi would leave his palace, alone, without an escort, for the house of one of his generals, Sisine, who was unmarried. A ladder would be lowered for him and the king would clamber up to the general. He would stay there for four hours before returning to the palace. This intrigue did not pass unobserved. Someone who was watching must have recognised him. – 'So it's true what they say. He goes out at night.' A report was left with the tribunal, where someone called the Pleader of Memphis attempted to speak; but the Pleader's voice was drowned by singers and musicians who refused to stop whistling and screaming. These disturbers of the peace had been sent by the court (perhaps, one surmises, with the knowledge of the king). The poor Pleader was forced to leave, discouraged and in tears. [4]

We do not have the end of this story, and even the parts of it which are preserved are riddled with gaps. We may suppose that the Pleader of Memphis went to the temple of Ptah and that the god found means to stop the scandal. Perhaps it was now that authority decided to forbid such practices throughout the kingdom, and especially in Memphis. This was not the only tale in which this particular author tried to please his public by displaying the weaknesses of the great.

Pepi II's pyramid was called Neferkare-Men-ankh, 'Neferkare is steadfast in life': an appropriate name, since the pyramid housed a centenarian. It stands in the southern part of the necropolis of Memphis, as near as possible to the royal palace of the same name. It is almost completely ruined, as are the adjoining buildings, the reception temple, the rising causeway, and the temple of the cult, where the Service des Antiquités has collected some interesting fragments of bas-reliefs.

A Libyan family is shown similarly in the temple of Sahure. It is there purely to recall that the Libyans were, in law and in fact, subjects of the pharaoh. A number of men – acrobats – have set up a mast, and they are struggling to climb the bars which keep it vertical, as though trying to reach the basket on top of a greasy pole. They are wearing striped jackets, and they have a feather stuck in their hair. The name of this apparatus, *sehent*, designates the conical hut which seems inseparable from the god Min. It is often found with a pole stuck between a pair of horns. In memory of the time when the fertility god had not yet left the shores of the Red Sea and the land of Punt, a copy of this hut was set up near the king's pyramid. In another representation we see the king hunting. Somewhere else, again, he is receiving homage from his counsellors. If the monument were intact it would present a picture of the king's everyday life.[5] Now the pyramid is just a mound with blunted outlines. The walls inside were once covered with religious texts, most of which were like the ones Maspero and, later, Sethe discovered in the earlier pyramids: the

(*opposite*) Limestone relief from the tomb of Tjey, at Sakkara. Serving girls, personifying his estates, carry baskets filled with the produce of fields and orchards.
(*overleaf top left*) Funerary boats carried the deceased to the abode of the dead.
(*overleaf left and right*) Models were put in tombs to serve their masters in the other world. Here one roasts a duck and another carries a box of beer jars on her head.

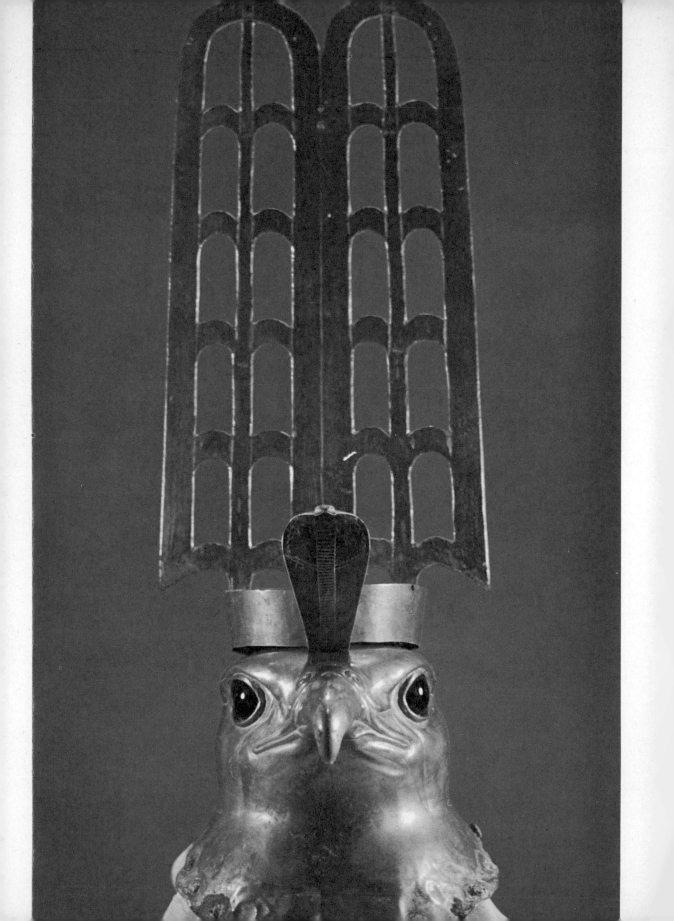

pyramids of Unis, Pepi I and Meryre. In their ignorance the thieves of ancient times believed that there were treasures hidden in the walls, and they made savage attacks on the texts. Naturally, they found nothing. (The same vandals violated the dark granite sarcophagus and wrecked the *serdab* where some statues were kept.) Recently, the archaeologist Jéquier collected, with infinite patience, all the tiny pieces of debris and restored them to their old places, thus 'reprinting' several chapters of what has been called the oldest book in the world.

I do not want to end this chapter on the last great king of the Old Kingdom without mentioning a work which is one of the masterpieces of the Cairo Museum – and, indeed, of all animal sculpture – the golden falcon head, found at Nekhen in 1897–8 (Hieraconpolis). The work was a wood and copper falcon, with its head and headdress made of gold and its eyes of obsidian. A royal image stood in front of the pedestal. The head is the most remarkable part. It has been burnished; the process of burnishing was invented in very ancient times, but it is more difficult to carry out on a head than on a simple vessel. Finally the head has been engraved. The ends of the obsidian bar set in the orbits have a quite extraordinary effect. The crown is poorly made, but when it is removed the head assumes a marvellous beauty and grandeur.

Circumstances do not allow us to date this masterpiece exactly, but all Egyptologists place it in dynasty VI. A little extra evidence could tip the balance in favour of Pepi II. Hieraconpolis is not very far from Elephantine and the Aswan cataract. And it was in the reign of Pepi II that the people of Aswan showed the greatest activity.

After Pepi II the history of Egypt is very obscure. The landed barons increased their power, and with the gradual independence of the nomes from a central authority, Egypt became resolved into the petty principalities of prehistoric times. It was the pharaohs of dynasty XI who reunited Egypt, and by the time of Amenemnes I we reach the height of the Middle Kingdom.

Head of a model falcon found at
Hieraconpolis, ancient Nekhen. The
uraeus and plumed crown symbolise
Horus, the city's patron deity.

2   The court of It-towe

Amenemnes I, first king of the court of It-towe

Amenemnes I is the founder of one of the most illustrious dynasties: dynasty XII, known in the Turin Papyrus as the Kings of the Residence of It-towe, a city on the border of the two lands (that is, of Upper and Lower Egypt). One cannot overemphasise the significance of Amenemnes' titulary. He took the terms *whm mswt*, 'the renewer of births', not only as his Horus name, but as his Nebti and Golden Horus names, which means that a family deprived of legitimate heirs, finished, and, perhaps, unpopular, had been replaced by another family, and the head of it already had his heirs.

We cannot identify the father or mother of Shetepibre Amenemhe, but it is very probable that his father was a vizier called Amenemnes, who, it is recorded, on one occasion went to the valley of Rohanu to bring back a fine slate slab as a cover for a sarcophagus. They spent about a fortnight in the famous valley. The quarriers' task was to slide a free-standing block of stone of about the right size into the valley. Their work was cut short by a gazelle which was clearly guided by the god Min. It showed no fear whatever of the men who were watching it, and it brought forth its young on the very stone they wanted. The men killed it, then recognised the episode as a miracle. They also had the good fortune – quite as providential – to find a well, completely unknown to those who frequented the valley, which provided them with fresh, pure water. They took measures to safeguard it, and returned in peace to Coptos after returning thanks to the god of Coptos, who was also the lord of the desert regions. Amenemnes retained a happy memory of his expedition, and, remembering a fine stone slab which he had noticed when he was vizier, he sent an expedition to bring it back to Egypt when he became king.

An important change dates from Amenemnes. Until his day the god Amun had had virtually no importance among the great gods of Egypt. Min reigned over Coptos; Monthu was lord of Thebes and, in a sense, the sponsor of the kings of the fallen dynasty, many of whom had called themselves Mentuhotep, 'Monthu is happy'. As the sponsor of the new king, Amun became the king of the gods. However, Amenemnes realised that if he stayed in Upper Egypt his

Painted wooden model, dating from dynasty x, of a company of Nubian
archers from the tomb of Mesehti at Aysut. The Nubians were not only the enemies
of Egypt, but also supplied them with mercenary soldiers.

authority over the Delta would be precarious. That was why he chose It-towe as his capital and took care to remember the gods of the Delta in the distribution of royal favours. At Dedit he built a temple in honour of Ba-Neb-Ded, whom the Greeks would know as Mendes. In the city of the god Set (who was far from honoured by many Egyptians), he built a temple dedicated to 'Ptah-who-is-at-the-south-of-his-wall', as if he wanted to win the favour of the god who was the patron of jubilees: in other words, to reign for at least thirty years.

Fate has preserved only a few royal effigies for us. A rather fine statue was found a few years ago at Dedamun in the Delta; it is not in bad condition, but without the nose one can hardly appreciate the sovereign's face. There is also another statue which has been known for a long time. It is broken into several pieces, but the head is not too badly damaged. As Maspero has observed, its expression seems quite benevolent, even if the features are rather soft, but this good-nature could very well hide subtlety and *savoir-faire*.

Amenemnes was not a great warrior, but he was a good politician. He had found Egypt divided and disorganised. Nebtowere, his immediate predecessor, who reigned for only two years, recruited his workmen in a region between the fifth and ninth nomes of Upper Egypt, and we do not know if his power went beyond these limits. Amenemnes consulted the old registers in order to define the boundaries of each nome by frontier stelae. When at last the old boundaries were re-established, there was an end to the wars which had devastated the country and hindered trade and food supplies. Peace also

A model group from the tomb of Nefu, showing workers in a brewery and a slaughterhouse.

brought a fair distribution of the water of the Nile, without which there could be only poor harvests.

It was quite as necessary to end the Asiatic invasions, for they caused terror and ruin in the eastern Delta – and even, perhaps, as far as Memphis. The kings of the Old Kingdom had organised punitive expeditions, penetrating a long way into Asia. They had even built a fortress, Qem-Ur, 'the Great Black One', in the isthmus, which they used as a base.[1] No doubt Qem-Ur was in ruins when Amenemnes assumed power and no longer served its purpose, any more than did the other fortresses which rose along the frontier as far as the Roads of Horus. Amenemnes was to choose a way of ending the invasions which was in conformity with his character, defensive rather than aggressive. He built the Prince's Wall to prevent the Aamu from pouring into Egypt. Henceforward they would have to beg for water for their animals according to the old custom.

There is no apparent trace of the Prince's Wall, any more than there is of the fortress of Qem-Ur or the others. An aerial survey might help us to find them again. For the moment we have to fall back on hypotheses. It has been suggested that the Prince's Wall covered the eastern frontier from Heliopolis to Pelusium. But there was no need for it there, because the Tumilat Wady was the usual route for troops who were going from Egypt to Syria, or from Syria to Egypt. The experiences of Sinuhe, a fugitive who left Egypt in the time of Sesostris I, the successor to Amenemnes I, proved that a single person could leave the country without any serious obstacle, avoiding the soldiers who were on guard. The Prince's Wall was therefore in the nature of a stronghold, possibly very important, built along the Tumilat Wady, but on the Egyptian rather than the Asian side. It was built near cultivated ground so that its defenders could receive help and fresh victuals in case of need. A hymn to Sesostris III seems to place this fortification near the city of Geshem in the nome of Soped.[2]

The re-organisation of the administration and the building of a stronghold to protect the Delta from the Barbarians were two acts which were doubtless carried out early in the reign. To men of letters and influential people, who could create discontent and perhaps revolution, the skilful king presented them both as acts of providence which the gods had foretold to a prophet in the days of Snofru the beneficent. The choice of Snofru was clever in itself, for Snofru, too, was the founder of a dynasty who was in no way destined by birth to sit on the throne of Horus.

The story was spread around that Snofru had informed his courtiers that he wanted to hear a fine speaker, and the courtiers had sung the praises of an upright man from Heliopolis, who was in charge of the rites of the goddess Bastet. This man of honour, who was called Neferti, had prophesied a sad time for the country, which would be ruined by foreigners, civil discord, and hostile elements:

But behold a king will come from the south, and his name will be Ameny. He will be the son of a woman of Ta-sti [the nome of Aswan and the regions further south], a child of Khen-Nekhen [the whole of Upper Egypt]. He will receive the White Crown. He will protect the Red Crown. He will unite the two powers [on his head] . . . The son of a man from the oriental delta will make himself a name for all eternity. Those who were disposed to evil, and meditated aggression, will be silent out of fear of him. The Asiatics will fall from terror of him, the Tjemeh will fall before his flame. The Prince's Wall will be built and the Aamu will no longer pour into Egypt. They will have to beg for water according to custom, so that their flocks may drink. Righteousness will be restored, and iniquity will be cast out . . .[3]

The seer refrained from naming the parents of the saviour-king, and instead of referring to him by name he used a sort of derivative, rather as the subjects of Ramses II, a little later, would call their master Sesesu. Perhaps this shows a sort of irony which is not disrespectful; it certainly comes well from the mouth of a man inspired by the gods. One can imagine that when the words of the prophet were spread through Egypt, those round the king and the powerful men in the provinces nodded their heads in approval and understanding.

In the year 20, after a busy reign, the king – who was already old – decided to share power with his eldest son Sesostris. This association of father and son was not yet traditional, but there had been precedents and it was accepted without any trouble. The king saw a further advantage in it: the consolidation of his dynasty. An elder son, already enthroned, should find no difficulty in being crowned.

The sharing of functions was natural, as Sinuhe said to the prince of Retjnu. The king in his palace would read the despatches and take decisions, while his son led the troops to where disorders and revolts occurred, in the east, west or south. This association lasted ten years and it might have lasted longer if the court of It-towe had not included hasty people who would benefit by change. One fine evening, as the king was taking a little rest before giving himself over to sleep, he heard a great commotion outside his door and assassins burst into his room. They may have been people whom he trusted, for Amenemnes made no resistance.

His son was in Libya at the time, leading an army against the Tjehnyu and the Tjemeh. Informed of events by loyal friends, he left the army immediately, and flew like a falcon to prevent someone from ascending the Horus throne even before the mourning was over. But the conspirators had sent an envoy to the army where another royal son held a command. What was said in the course of this conversation? Of course we do not know, but it was something so serious that Sinuhe, who had chanced to overhear it, saw fit not only to escape, but to leave Egypt altogether.

No doubt the assassins warned the second royal son of the murder, and asked him to go to the capital and forestall his elder brother. May one offer some theories to complement the brief texts? Manetho tells us that

Amenemnes ii was assassinated by eunuchs. Could he perhaps have made a mistake in the king's number?[4] If the assassins were eunuchs, the instigator of the assassination might have been a wife of Amenemnes i. The first royal wife, the mother of Sesostris, was dead or relegated to the background, and the king had a younger wife, but the latter might have wanted to see her own child on the throne.

However that may be, the plot failed. Sesostris was recognised as king, and no one seriously contested his legitimacy. Were the conspirators punished, and if so, how? We know nothing about it. But Sesostris summoned a man of letters to affirm his authority; and this man of letters composed a text which has remained one of the classics of Egyptian literature, of which many copies were made on papyrus and ostraca. This man of letters was the scribe Khety, the author of *The Satire of Professions*. His new work was called *The Teaching of Amenemnes in Fifteen Verses*. The words are put into Amenemnes' mouth, and he speaks as if he were still alive. And of course he was still alive, though in the world of Osiris, and still perfectly capable of advising his successor and of intervening directly in Egyptian affairs.

After a brief show of defiance towards subordinates and usurpers, Amenemnes continues: 'One can only count on oneself. On the day of tragedy there are no allies. He himself, who had succoured the poor and the orphan, only reaped ingratitude and hostility.' And then he comes to the drama:

Woken by the noise of fighting, he did not even have time to cry out that he bequeathed his power to his absent son. No doubt he lacked foresight. He did not know that his palace sheltered traitors. But his work bears witness for him. He visited Elephantine and the Delta as the kings his ancestors had done in the Old Kingdom. Order was re-established at home. The Nubians and the Asiatics were cast back at the frontiers. A fine palace was built.
[The last verses mention Sesostris, to whom the king gives a few further counsels.]

The Beatty iv Papyrus contains a eulogy by the scribe Khety: he drew up *The Teaching* after the king had rested in peace and returned to heaven and entered among the Masters of the Necropolis.

We have no reason to accuse any particular person in the household, though of course we only know the household imperfectly. What is certain is that Sesostris returned in time to take charge of things again, and that he imposed court mourning – as we see at the beginning of Sinuhe – and concerned himself with the funeral of the king, who had already raised his own pyramid near Lisht, very near the palace of It-towe. The pyramid is called Amenemnes in Ka-Nefru, and King Nefru's own daughter was called the Royal Daughter of the Amenemnes Pyramid in Ka-Nefru. Instead of giving herself as the daughter of her father's flesh, she was following a custom established since the time of Unis by giving herself as the Daughter of the

Royal Pyramid, that is, not as a creature of perishable flesh, but as part of something built to last for eternity.[5] The monument in the Marseilles Museum, which we have already mentioned, clearly shows the role attributed to the pyramid. King Teti, who, like Pepi II, belongs to dynasty VI, is not represented lying in his sarcophagus: he is represented standing erect in the middle of his pyramid, and it is as a living being that he is receiving the homage of the faithful.

The pyramid of Amenemnes is ruined today, it is just a sort of tumulus, but people have been able to make out the plan. The kings had by this time abandoned the gigantic monuments which had been the glory of dynasty IV; the average height of the buildings was now only about one hundred and eighty feet.[6] However, that was enough to attract the attention of travellers passing the palace of Sesostris; and, when he grew old, Sesostris in turn raised his pyramid near his father's.

Amenemnes III, builder of the Labyrinth

Between the death of Amenemnes I and the accession of Amenemnes III there stretched a period of about a hundred and twenty years. During this time Sesostris I, Amenemnes II, Sesostris II and Sesostris III succeeded each other to the throne of Horus. If we want to picture the state of Egypt during this period, and especially towards the end, we find ourselves confronted by contradictory texts. If we believe the author of the hymn to Sesostris III, or the unknown author of a *Book of Wisdom* which seems to have enjoyed great popularity, or the *Advices of a man to his son*, Egypt was happy and prosperous during this period. The power of the pharaoh was so great that everyone was obliged to serve him with all his strength and with all his will. – 'Do this, it will be salutary, you will find it to your advantage all your days.' And yet the pharaoh and his court may not have been as sure of the future as his censer-bearers would have us believe. For at the same time, other texts reveal that there were neighbouring peoples and princes, and even subjects of the pharaoh in Egypt itself, who were ready to revolt, who fought and threatened to fight. It is astonishing to find that these lists include most of the cities of Palestine and Syria and their leaders, as well as the people of the South, and the Tjehnyu and the Tjemeh, two peoples of the West.[1] The Egyptians who are listed alongside these alleged enemies receive the same malediction as they do.

The use of magic did not prevent the pharaohs from employing other means of defence which had been successfully used. As we have seen,

Funerary stele of a royal herdsman, shown presenting a sheaf of lotus flowers to the lion-headed goddess Sekhmet.

Amenemnes I built the Prince's Wall east of the Delta to prevent the Aamu from pillaging the Delta. In the South, the pharaohs pushed the frontiers back from the First to the Second Cataract and raised mighty strongholds in the neighbourhood, at Mergissa and Semna. But what was the use of walls and fortresses if the defenders lacked courage? Sesostris III held very clear views on the subject which he expressed in vigorous terms in the stela of the year XVI found at Semna:

The year XVI, the 3rd month of the winter, the 1st, My Majesty created a frontier in the land of Heh.
I have created a frontier exceeding that of my fathers. I have given more than was given to me. I am a king who speaks and acts. That which my heart has conceived, my arm performs. I am aggressive in attack and resolute in success. Words do not sleep in my heart ... I attack if I am attacked; I am silent if people are silent. I answer a word according to its implications. Those who stay silent when they are attacked embolden the adversary. It is the act of a valiant man to take the offensive. It is the act of a coward to escape. It is that of a real [here is a word which defies transcription] to remain on one's frontier.

After some very harsh judgments on the Nubians, the king ends with an adjuration to his successors:

The son who guards my frontiers is the son My Majesty will recognise, but he who refuses to fight for me will not be my son. I would not know him. That is why My Majesty has set up my likeness on this frontier which My Majesty has made, so that you should be steadfast and fight for me.[2]

When Amenemnes, third of the name, was crowned king, he took as his Horus name 'Great in Power'; he took as his forename Ni-Maat-Re, 'Re is in possession of the truth'. Contemporaries and Greek authors often refer to the kings of Egypt by their forenames rather than their names. They transcribed Ni-Maat-Re as Labares, which is correct, but they also transcribed it as Ismandes and Moiris or Moeris. However different these names may appear, they all derive from Nemare and refer to the same person.

Nemare was certainly not old at the time of his accession, for he reigned at least forty-six years, and few of the pharaohs reached or exceeded the age of sixty-five. Let us say he was twenty or so at his coronation. We are certainly reminded of a young man of twenty when we look at the beautiful statue found at Hawwara. The sculptor has taken great care with the face, which often happens in Egyptian art, which captures extremely well the young king's gaiety, his frivolity, one might even say his mischievousness. Perhaps the pharaoh was thinking about love, about sports such as hunting, perhaps about war itself, provided that it was bold and joyous and free from the horrors which usually go with it. It seems there was no cloud to darken his horizon.

The god Thoth, pouring a libation of
the water of life over Queen
Hatshepsut. Her figure, originally on
the left, was erased by Thutmose III.

(*above*) Amenemnes III when young. He was the last great king of his dynasty and ruled for fifty years. Afterwards there was a general decline ending with the Hyksos invasion.

(*opposite*) Sesostris I was a great builder, he not only founded a new temple at Heliopolis, but built or rebuilt on sites all over Egypt.

There are other statues, no doubt sculpted early in the reign, which are not very different from the masterpiece at Hawwara; but others show the king more advanced in age. On the Leningrad and Moscow statues, the features and the shape of the face are the same, but the gaiety seems to have gone. This impression is confirmed by three statues found in the burial place at Karnak, (now exhibited at the Cairo Museum as numbers 42015, 42016 and 42020). These statues show a king who has grave problems on his mind. As for statue number 42014, which comes from the same source, it shows a man who is weary, bent and worn. Perhaps it is worry and sorrow, rather than the passing years, which have hollowed his cheeks and weighed down his eyelids. How can one explain this contrast? I do not think the Egyptian armies had suffered reverses, or that there had been a plot against the king's life. Certainly the records say nothing about it. In the year 44, Amenemnes IV was associated with the king, but this sort of association was customary during dynasty XII. This should not have worried him.

During his reign, the turquoise mines continued to be exploited as before. At Byblos, relations were closer than ever between the pharaoh and the local king, who was then called Abichemu. This personage had been accorded the title of prince, which made him the equal of the highest-ranking Egyptians when he came to the court of It-towe to arrange commercial exchanges. According to recent discoveries which have been made at Byblos, he had very ample means. He also had a perfect knowledge of the Egyptian language and script, and had hieroglyphic inscriptions carved on his monuments. When he died, Amenemnes III granted him the royal offering since he ranked as a prince. The offering consisted of several objects of value, the most remarkable being an obsidian vase set with gold, marked with the name of the pharaoh Nemare, and containing an unguent of the finest quality.[3] In doing this Amenemnes III only continued the policy of his predecessors. His claims to glory lay elsewhere.

Since the days of the Old Kingdom, the Fayyum had attracted huntsmen and fishermen. The shores of the lake, which was then much vaster than it is today, lent themselves to cultivation. The Bahr Yusuf, which diverges from the Nile much further south, and irrigates the neighbouring desert lands throughout the year, is forced by an undulation in the soil, just before El-Lahun, to flow towards the west. It rushes through a narrow creek in the Libyan chain and bursts into the lake. In a text of the Middle Empire, this province is called the 'pehu of the south'. A pehu was a natural reservoir as well as a place for hunting and fishing. Every nome had a pehu, but, thanks to its exceptional dimensions, the Fayyum was a pehu for the whole of southern Egypt. We know that Amenemnes III took an interest in the Fayyum, for many archaeological remains which bear his name have been found in the Kiman Fares.[4]

His interest in the Fayyum is also established by the account of a strong

This head of Amenemnes III when older,
contrasts with that on page 60 showing
the realism of Egyptian portraiture.

expedition which was sent to the Valley of Rohanu, in the desert between Coptos and the Red Sea, which brought back ten statues of five cubits destined for the building: 'Stable is the life of Amenemnes in the temple of Sopek and Chedit.' It was about this time that the pharaoh had an idea which might be described as original: he thought of completing the work of nature so that the lake might hold the excess inundation, preventing it from flooding the neighbouring lands and giving it back to the Nile when the farmers needed water (Strabo xvi, 37). The two ends of the canal (continues Strabo) were therefore closed by flood-gates. Herodotus had already noted that the water was brought from the Nile and flowed into the lake for six months, and that it flowed out for six months. What modern engineers have achieved with the massive means at their disposal south of Aswan, already existed in the Fayyum in a more modest form under dynasty xii.

The Labyrinth was Nemare's second claim to glory, and the building of it was no doubt a result of the work on Lake Moeris. Most authors believed that the Labyrinth was the king's funerary temple. However, the existing temples, like the antechamber of the pyramid, are essentially monuments of the royal cult. The events of the reign are recorded there; the king is represented in the company of the gods, receiving offerings from his dominions. As far as one can judge from the classical authors – for its site is only a field of ruins – the Labyrinth was a public building.

The Labyrinth was a collection of palaces, and behind the palaces there were as many chapels as there were nomes in Egypt. These chapels were lined up (says Strabo) and divided (says Herodotus) into two rows, separated by a courtyard. According to Strabo, the deputations from each nome went to the Labyrinth to sacrifice together and to pass solemn judgment on questions of high importance. Each deputation was led to the chapel which represented the particular deputation's nome.

This passage in Strabo is very revealing, especially since the White Chapel has been reconstructed at Karnak through the efforts of Chevrier. The base of this monument is virtually an administrative geography of Egypt; on one side are the nomes of the South, on the other are the nomes of the North; there is a record for every nome, telling us its emblem, its area, the name of the capital, and the names of its gods. The Labyrinth was, on a huge scale, the equivalent of the White Chapel and similar monuments; but instead of restricting themselves to a few essential pieces of information, the builders had to record on the walls everything about the nomes; especially the frontiers, the water rights, the taxes, cults and monuments. And so, in a sense, the inhabitants of the nomes came to refresh their memories and to find out the extent of their rights and their obligations towards the king.

What surprised the Greeks, what made Strabo say that the Labyrinth almost equalled the pyramids, and what made Herodotus say that it even surpassed them, was the immensity of the monument. The slabs that formed

Relief from Karnak showing Sesostris I and the god Ptah, the creator, embracing inside a shrine at Memphis.

the roof were so vast that standing on them they felt as if they were on a stone plain. And then there was the complexity of the rooms, joined to each other by such an inextricable maze of galleries that a stranger could not go round them without a guide.

Let us sum up what we have learnt about Lake Moeris and the Labyrinth. They were both the work of the same king, Moeris, that is to say Amenemnes III. Lake Moeris is a vast pehu; it can take in the waters which the Bahr Yusuf brings in the flood, holding the water and returning it when the farmers need it. The Labyrinth is a building in which everything the Egyptians needed to know was engraved on stone. Every time a disagreement arose between neighbouring nomes, or between a nome and the people of the central administration, they would turn to the record in the Labyrinth which supplied the answer: an answer established on the basis of the ancient records, carefully summarised by the best archivists. The name Labyrinth has itself aroused the curiosity of scholars. Someone tried to explain it by inventing an expression like Ra-per Rahenit, which, one might add, is not to be found in the texts. There is no doubt that the second half of the word Labyrinth comes directly from the Egyptian Ra-henit. An expression like 'The king [or the god N] has founded [or delights in] Ra-henit', such as the Egyptian texts of the Middle Kingdom give us, could have produced the Greek word Labyrinth. No authentic trace of the Labyrinth itself has come down to us.

There are two pyramids attributed to Amenemnes III, one at Dahshur and the other in the Fayyum. The first, the 'black pyramid', is built of unburnt brick, and does not seem to have been used by the king. Since the pharaohs generally built their pyramid near the palace they lived in, we can assume that Amenemnes III lived at It-towe in the beginning of his reign, like his predecessors. That is why he raised a pyramid of unburnt brick at Dahshur, in the region of Memphis. Its little crowning pyramid has been found: it is

made of wonderfully smooth black granite.[5] There are inscriptions in fine hieroglyphics guaranteeing the king the protection of Harakhte and an excellent reception in the Mountain of the West.

At a date which we cannot specify, Amenemnes III adopted the habit of living at the Fayyum, to keep a closer supervision over the great works at Lake Moeris, the embellishments of the temple of Sobek, and the building of the Labyrinth. He then had a new pyramid built at the corner of the Labyrinth.[6] Though the architects took the greatest precautions to hide the vault from despoilers, vandals got in and removed the coffin, only leaving the quartzite sarcophagus.

It is therefore not actually proved that the king was buried at Hawwara, but it is extremely probable. A number of small tombs were built in the enclosure of the pyramid at Dahshur; one of them was used by King Hor, whom the Turin Papyrus places in dynasty XIII. Egyptologists have been divided about this sovereign. Some keep to the indications on the Turin Papyrus, others maintain that King Hor's coffer of vases is sealed in the name of Nemare, which makes this sovereign an associate of Amenemnes III. In antiquity, however, a king's seal was sometimes used after his death. It is therefore not proved, and I myself do not think that Amenemnes III had an associate. On his death the throne of Horus fell to another Amenemnes, the fourth, who reigned eight years. Amenemnes IV continued to exploit the turquoise mines and, like his predecessor, sent valuable gifts to King Ypchemuabi, the son and successor of Abichemu.

But the days of the court of It-towe were numbered. After the brief reign of Sebeknofru, the power changed hands and Egypt disintegrated economically and politically. Perhaps Amenemnes III had sensed that his family and all Egypt were to fall on evil days and the sculptors of Karnak had caught these forebodings.

(*opposite*) Wall-painting, showing girls playing a ball game, from the tomb of Chnum-hotep at Beni Hasan.

(*right*) Scene of men feeding antelopes in Chnum-hotep's tomb. He held the position of Governor of the Eastern Desert.

3 The flowering of a dynasty

Kamose, one of the liberators of Egypt

King Kamose is an unfamiliar sovereign to everybody but professional Egyptologists, but he has an incontestable claim to glory. He undertook the liberation of Egypt, which had been occupied for over a century by the Hyksos. Under a certain King Tutimaios, we read in Josephus (who is quoting Manetho) :[1]

> The divine anger blew against us, and suddenly, from the east, a people of unknown race had the audacity to invade our land. They took possession of it by force, without difficulty and without even having to fight. They captured our leaders, savagely set fire to our cities, and razed the temples of the gods to the ground. They treated the natives with the utmost cruelty, cutting the throats of some and taking the wives and children of others as slaves. [Against Apion 1, 75–65]

How could such a disaster have happened? If the Egyptians had been moved by the feelings which Sesostris III had expressed with such conviction, the calamity would certainly not have occurred. But Sesostris' successor, Amenemnes III, was already more concerned with enriching his country than with its defence, and the kings of what we call dynasty XIII were in general completely incompetent.

Who were these people called the Hyksos? The name comes from the same source as the preceding text, and in Egyptian it is transcribed as Nega Khasut, 'Sheikh of foreign lands'. These Hyksos, so often mentioned, were none other than the Aamu, who had long been known to the Egyptians. A king has left an unflattering likeness of them:

> As for the vile Aamu, wretched is the land in which he lives. In its waters is calamity, in its many woods lies secrecy. The roads in the land of the Aamu are impassable because of the mountains. The Aamu cannot stay where he is. His feet are always moving. He has fought since the time of the god without being victor or vanquished. He does not announce the day of his fight, he is like a man who is about to do a foul deed . . . Yet be not anxious about him . . . He will pillage an isolated isba; he will not overcome a populous city.

Opinion differs about dating the Sphinx at Giza, but it is now generally regarded as dynasty XIX.

The name Aamu corresponds, letter for letter, with the name of the Arabs, and the description suits them perfectly. We shall therefore use either name, as we choose.

When these Hyksos or Aamu invaders were tired of looting, they began to think about ruling Egypt. They set up kings who more or less aped the pharaohs. They had a capital, Avaris, an old city of theologians (it would later be called Tanis). They adopted Set as their national god: Set, who, of all the Egyptian gods, is the one most like Baal. They found themselves allies south of Aswan. Although they dealt cautiously with some of the Egyptians, especially Egyptians who honoured Set, they acquired landed estates and movable property. We have some idea of these kings from Egyptian texts. Towards the end they were called Khayan, and there were three Apopi distinguished from each other by their forenames: Nebkehepeshre, Akenenre, and Aweserre.

For a time these invaders may have occupied the whole of Egypt, but finally resistance was organised and the southern nomes, beginning with Cusae, shook off their yoke to give their allegiance to local princes.

The Hyksos king, Akenenre, decided to provoke his contemporary at Thebes – a king whose name was Sekenenre, very similar to his own. He had already had a brief inscription in bad hieroglyphics engraved on some of the finest statues in the temple of Avaris: – 'The good god Akenenre, son of the Sun Apopi, given by the life beloved of Set.' Finally he sent the prince of Thebes a direct provocation. We are informed about this by a text which has often been commented on, a text which some modern scholars consider to have no historical value:

While the land of Egypt was in misery and there was no king, Life, Health, Strength, King Apopi, who served no other god but Set and had just built him a temple beside his palace, sent the prince of Thebes a message the tenor of which had been suggested by scribes: 'Keep away from the pool of the hippopotami to the east of your city, for they prevent sleep from coming to me day or night. The noise they make fills the citizens' ears'.[2]

It was a joke. How could the hippopotami, frolicking in a lake near Thebes, be heard by the people of the prince of Avaris, nearly six hundred miles away? But we must remember that the sovereigns of antiquity sent one another riddles – Solomon was a past master at the game. Sekenenre consulted the great soothsayer at his court, but as the account here breaks off, we do not know what happened next. Possibly the result was war. Certainly Prince Sekenenre's mummy bears traces of many wounds.

But now we come to firmer ground. Ahhotpe, Sekenenre's wife, had given him two sons, Kamose and Ahmose. It is the elder son, Kamose, we are concerned with. Three records, which have appeared in succession, have greatly improved our knowledge of his reign. The first is a wooden tablet with an historic text on one side and a sapiential text on the other;[3] then there is a broken stele[4] and finally another stele which is intact.[5] It has been proved that the tablet and the broken stele bore the same text which recorded what had happened at the beginning of Kamose's reign.

The king summoned his council and explained the situation to them; it was far from hopeful:

I know what my courage is for. There is a king [literally a great man] at Avaris, and there is another at Cush. I am sitting like a hyphen between an Arab and a Nubian. Those who dwell in the black land share their possessions with me. I cannot make him cross at Memphis the water of Egypt; now he is in possession of Khmunu (Hermopolis). There is no one left who is not overwhelmed by the taxes of the Asiatics. I am going to meet him to cleave his belly. It is in my heart to deliver Egypt and to strike the Arabs.

This was clear enough. The councillors understood perfectly, and the bellicose talk was not to their liking.

The great men on the council spoke out:

Serving girls and a guest at a banquet, depicted on a wall painting in the tomb chapel of Djeserkareseneb, which dates from the reign of Thutmose IV.

Teti-Sheri, daughter of a commoner,
and grandmother of Kamose and
Ahmose.

Chons, son of Amun and Mut, was god
of the moon and science.

Mut, the great mother, was goddess of
Thebes and wife of Amun.

Behold, the water of the Arabs flows as far as Cusae. The finest of their fields are tilled for us. Our oxen are in the marshes. The wheat is sent to our pigs. Our oxen are not taken. Let him have the land of the Arabs. We shall have the black land. If he attacks us, then we shall fight against him.

In fact the councillors believed that there should be no action. There was no lack of anything, there was even wheat for the pigs, and their oxen were watering in the marshes. These views scarcely conformed with the king's who already saw himself acclaimed as a liberator throughout Egypt:

I went down the river like a champion to overthrow the Arabs, by the order of Amun, who is just in his undertakings. My valiant soldiers went before me like the burning flame. The archers of the Medjayu [auxiliaries] left the fortresses to challenge the Asiatics and lay their places low. The East and the West gave me their fatness, my army was well provided with everything. . . . I did not let [anyone] escape . . .

Once on the move, the army, which was composed of Medjayu, met no resistance until it reached Nefrusy, the stronghold of Middle Egypt, where Teti son of Pepi (or Apepi) had entrenched himself. It is strange to see the names of the old national sovereigns used by the chiefs of the Hyksos. They were not allowed to escape. Then came the day of the assault:

I spent the night in my boat, my heart was happy. The earth grew light. I was on the enemy like a falcon. In the time it takes to scent the mouth, I assailed him, I brought down his walls, I massacred his men. I made his women come down on the quay. My soldiers were like lions with their prey, taking their share of people, herds, milk, fat and honey . . .

But the capture of Nefrusy was unimportant. 'Another place was deserted when we reached it. The enemy chariots had abandoned the city.' (This is our earliest record of the use of drawn carts.) At this point the text breaks off, and we do not know the immediate result of this first success.

King Kamose celebrated his victory with two stelae: they are written in the same way, and they may have been set up beside each other in the temple of Karnak. The second stela is intact. It was discovered being used as a foundation under a statue, and in better times it must have stood in a court-yard of the temple of Amun. It begins, very abruptly, in an ironic style, with a declaration of war; and, in a way which is sometimes obscure for the modern reader, provocations, invective and predictions are mingled together. Kamose already sees himself as the master of Avaris, and he considers his enemy to be completely routed. Some commentators have even believed that Kamose really captured the enemy capital. But that only happened under Ahmose, his successor, and we shall see this clearly when Kamose comes to the actual facts. 'One sees your vile back when my soldiers are behind you. The women of Avaris no longer conceive, and their hearts no longer beat in

(*opposite above*) Jewellery of dynasty XVIII: beads of faience and carnelian; rings of jasper, faience and gold; a gold mounted lapis lazuli scarab and tiny gold figures of gods.
(*opposite below*) Model of a goat-headed god, possibly an aspect of the god Set.

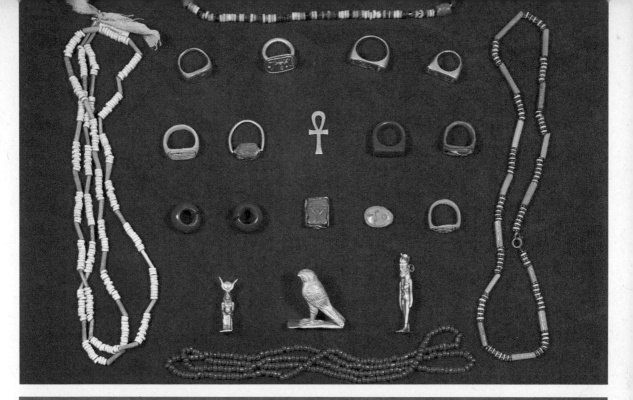

their breasts when they hear my soldiers' war-cries.' As usual, the pharaoh is another Horus, and his soldiers are themselves like falcons. On the other hand, the soldiers of Avaris are cowards, and their leaders only want to hide themselves. As for the pharaoh's natural ally, the King of Retjnu, he is in no hurry at all to fight it out, and he prudently remains in his own domains.
Let Kamose speak again:

I noticed his wife [the wife of the king of Avaris] on his terraces, she was looking through the openings over the quay. I saw them peeping over the walls, like owlets in their hole . . .
Here I am, I have come, my deed is fortunate, good luck is with me . . .
I swear by Amun. I do not swear by you. I shall not let you oppress my lands again. I am not upon your lips [the Hyksos king no longer swears by the pharaoh]. Your heart is mistaken there, vile Aamu. Here I am drinking the wine of your vineyards, which the Aamu, my prisoners, have pressed for me.
I am destroying the place of your residence. I shall cut down your trees. I shall cast your women [into the bottom of my boats]. I shall take your chariots.

And then there is a passage which anticipates events. Kamose already sees himself master of the water of Avaris, free to appropriate the new pinewood ships, three hundred in number, and also to appropriate a splendid booty of gold, silver, lapis-lazuli and turquoise, as well as innumerable axes, oil, resin, fat, honey – in fact all the precious woods and useful products of Retjnu.

I have taken everything at once and left nothing. Avaris is laid waste. O vile Aamu who repeated 'I am a lord without peer from Khmunu [Hermopolis, in Middle Egypt] to Pi-Hathor [near Ismailiya], by way of Avaris which is on the Nile.' I have destroyed all that. There is no one there [to stop me]. I have destroyed their cities, their cellars are a ruin which will be red for all eternity because of the evil they have done to Egypt, I shall make them hear the cry of the Aamu who have offended Egypt their mistress.

We may learn several valuable things from these invectives. First of all that the Hyksos invasion really happened (several historians have denied or minimised it). The invasion stretched from the old frontier as far as Khmunu. Avaris was the royal residence, Apopi, the Hyksos king, was on good terms with the king of Syria, and pinewood ships, which were evidently built at Byblos, brought the essential victuals and additional supplies to the city.
It certainly seems that the prince of Thebes proceeded with a quick attack on Nefrusy, and perhaps it was in answer to Apopi's reproaches that he sent these invectives.
Now we come to the realm of facts. Kamose had not been wrong when he complained to his council that he was squashed between the Asiatics and the Nubians. He knew the dangers of waging war on two fronts. As soon as things began to go badly, Aweserre, king of Avaris, son of the Sun Apopi, sent

The Temple of Amun at Karnak: in the front are the remains of a colossus of Thutmose II, behind is the hypostyle hall of Ramses II.

a message to the king of Cush, reproaching him for his inaction just when Kamose was attacking his territory.

I did not provoke him after the manner of all he had done against you. He has chosen two countries to their misfortune: mine and yours. He has laid them waste. He is coming down the river, do not linger. While he is [warring] against me here, no one in Egypt will stop you and rise against you. And we shall share the cities of Egypt between us.

It was a splendid programme, but, unfortunately for the king of Avaris, the bearer of the message was captured by Kamose's soldiers. And Kamose did not hide his happiness, which he felt he had deserved.

All happy and lost in joy is King Wadj-Kheperre the chastiser of faults. I have caused the foreign lands and [all] the earth to submit to me, and the Nile likewise . . . No one can find the path which escapes me. I have not neglected my soldiers. I have taken nothing from the land of the man who respects me. I have come down the river to fight you. We have found him [?], he saw our beacon, he was running from the land of Cush to find his position.

I captured [the messenger] on the road. I did not let him attain his end, but when I had taken him, my strength struck into his heart and destroyed his body, for his messengers told him what I had done in the district of the Black Dog which was in his dominions.

I shall send out a troop of warriors to ravage the oasis of Bahriya, to ensure that no one rebels against me while I am at Saka.

We need only glance at the map to appreciate what had happened. After the capture of Nefrusy, a messenger had taken the desert route, from oasis to oasis, to carry the king of the Hyksos' letter to the king of Cush. After capturing him, Kamose set him free again to take the news to his master; and, in order to forestall similar incidents, Egyptian soldiers were to ravage the oasis of Bahriya. In the meanwhile, Kamose would hold Saka, the city of Set in the nome of the Black Dog, a city which was known to be loyal to the king of Avaris, to forestall any attempt at aggression. Kamose did not take his advantage further. The inundation had begun, and it stopped operations. The king, who had suffered no losses, went to rest at Asyut. He was acclaimed by the whole population, who were happy to see the end of their miseries.

No doubt the liberation had only just begun. Memphis, Heliopolis and other famous cities were still in enemy hands. We do not know whether Kamose had the joy of entering Memphis, we do not even know how much longer he still had to live. Did he die a natural death? Did he die fighting? It has been claimed that there were two Kamoses, but this has not been proved. It was reserved for his brother Ahmose to complete the great work, to repel the Hyksos and the Nubians, and to raise a magnificent victory stela.

Kamose spent his last years preparing his tomb, like his ancestors, the kings

An obelisk of Thutmose III originally erected at Karnak or Heliopolis, and now in Istanbul.

and princes of dynasty XVII, at the foot of the hills of Dra'Abu'N-Naga.[6]
Towards the middle of the last century, some of the Khedive's workmen,
looking for gold, discovered the burial-place of Queen Ahhotpe, wife of
Sekenenre the brave and mother of Kamose. The sarcophagus which they found
there was gilded all over and contained some magnificent things. Mariette, the
French Egyptologist, was informed of the find at the last moment. He inter-
cepted the moudhir's boat and, by menace and persuasion, obtained the
custody of the jewels in exchange for a receipt. However, it was a serious
matter, for he had forcibly removed some packages which were destined for
high circles. He therefore hastened to Alexandria, where he told his tale so
amusingly that he managed to make the Pasha laugh. The Pasha kept only a
gold chain for one of his wives and a few jewels (which he soon returned), and
so it was that a fascinating collection came to be in the Boulaq Museum. Most
of the things, indeed the finest of them, had been executed in workrooms in
the time of Kamose, or a little earlier. Others were later added to them,
things which came from the pharaoh Ahmose, like the axe decorated with a
griffin and a likeness of the king slaying a Hyksos, with other axes and daggers.

Kamose's share seems rather feeble in comparison. It includes a votive
barge with its crew of oarsmen set on a four-wheeled chariot, and a fan handle
worked in gold. There was already a state axe in the Evans Collection.

Kamose, the son of a warrior king, Sekenenre the brave, was himself a brave
man, and he in turn produced other warriors. He did not lack enthusiasm and
had a real talent for imprecation. Dynasty XVII handsomely comes to an end
with him in about 1580 BC.

Makare Hatshepsut, a great queen

When we talk of the queens of Egypt, it is nearly always a question of
princesses who were called royal daughters, then royal wives when they
married a pharaoh (often their brother), and finally royal mothers when they
gave birth to a child. All the same, they were not really queens, in the sense in
which, for example, we use the term when we mean the queen of England.
The titles by which the royal power was invested in the pharaoh did not apply
to them. As for the titles of royal daughter, wife or mother, they simply
recorded a state of things, and we cannot even say if they were granted
automatically or if there had to be a royal decree.

However, Egypt did have some queens in the proper sense of the word.

These queens had a proper protocol like the king. The years of their reign were counted from a coronation which was no less solemn than that of a pharaoh. There are three such queens: Queen Nitocris who ends dynasty VI, Queen Sebeknofrure who ends dynasty XII, and finally Hatshepsut, who is the subject of the present chapter. Hatshepsut did not earn renown on the battle-field but she has left us an imperishable monument which is justly called the 'Sublime of Sublimes', the temple of Der el-Bahri.

Thutmose I, the third sovereign of dynasty XVIII, had married his sister Ahmose, by whom he had two sons, Amenmose and Wadjmose, and a daughter, Hatshepsut. His successor, Thutmose II, was the child of a lesser queen named Mutnofre. When Thutmose II in turn became king, he followed a well-established custom and married his sister, Hatshepsut, who had only daughters. He had another wife, Isis, of obscure birth, by whom he had a son, Thutmose. When Thutmose II died after a reign which apparently did not last more than ten years, Prince Thutmose was very young to rule and despite the existence of a powerful party asserting his rights, he came to the throne only as a lesser partner of the royal daughter, the royal wife Hatshepsut. Her claim was strong, for she was the daughter of a king by his first wife, as well as being the wife of a king. Thutmose was a son, by a less important wife, of a father who was himself only the son of a lesser queen. Before many years had passed she had assumed the Double Crown and was no longer merely a queen as Nitocris and Sebeknofrure had been. As her Horus name she took Usert-Kau, mighty in *kas*; as Vulture-Cobra, Uadjit-Renpet, which means fresh in years; as Golden Horus, Netert-khau, divine in apparitions.

Her royal name, which is often used – indeed, more often used than her name of birth – is read as Makare on the monuments. We do not know how Prince Thutmose was treated, but there is good reason to believe that, if he had had any power, he would have usurped his aunt's place on the throne of Horus. When he finally became king, he attacked the queen's monuments in fury, defacing her names at Thebes and in the provinces. He tore down her statues and had them smashed into pieces and the fragments buried as deep as possible. Not deep enough, however. The mission from the New York Museum managed to find a good many of them and to restore them to their original appearance.[1]

In order to further her ambition, Makare made skilful use of a theory which had been put forward by certain theologians of the Old Kingdom. She maintained that her father, Thutmose I, had intended her to reign. However, this was not enough. On the walls of her temple, the Sublime of Sublimes, she had all the moments in this sacred drama recorded. Amun-Re, the king of gods, tells all the gods of the Great Enneade of his intention to give a sovereign to Egypt.[2] He assumes the appearance of the reigning king, Thutmose I and appears in the queen's presence on the night when Hatshepsut is conceived. All the gods take an interest in the mother and child. Chnum

A reconstructed drawing of the ram-headed god, Chnum the creator, modelling Hatshepsut on his wheel, with the god Thoth recording it.

models her on his potter's wheel; the same god, and the goddess Heqt, come to deliver Queen Ahmose and the heavenly cow feeds the child with its milk. Only the impious could have contested the rights of a queen so visibly protected by the gods. We may be sure that such impious people would have made their appearance if the queen had not surrounded herself with a constellation of eminent men, and entrusted them with the most important functions in the state. Among them were Hapu-Senb, first prophet of Amun, Thuty, Semna, and Min-Nekht, the chief of works. Min-Nekht was as capable of directing the excavation, transport and erection of two granite obelisks, as of building the sacred barge; he could build sanctuaries, or supervise the most delicate works of the goldsmith and cabinet-maker. It was these dignitaries, and others, who restored the temple of Hathor at Cusae, which had been completely neglected since the time of the Hyksos. Relations with Byblos flourished again as they had done in the days of Snofru and Amenemnes III. Once again the timber from the land of Nega was stacked on the quays at Thebes. The turquoise mines of Sinai were re-opened. Envoys to the southern lands negotiated the transport of metals and precious commodities, and panther skins and elephants' teeth were traded with the inhabitants of the Libyan coast.

All the pharaohs liked luxury, but no doubt Makare was even more

Bas-relief of Queen Hatshepsut drinking milk from the mother goddess, Hathor, who is here given the aspect of a cow.

exacting, and she demanded as much for the gods as she did for herself. I do not know if the kings of the Middle Kingdom were already in the habit of gilding obelisks, but all the upper part of the fine obelisk still standing, and that of its fellow, which has been pulled down and broken, were covered with gold; they illuminated the land like the sun.[3]

One dignitary in the queen's entourage stands entirely alone: the chief of chiefs of work, the royal chancellor, the grand steward Senenmut. The names of Senenmut and the queen are found together on several monuments, among them a rock at Aswan, a cenotaph, and foundation stones in the chapel of Hathor at Der el-Bahri. They are not associated as those of a sovereign and her subject, but more like two people of the same rank, almost, one ventures to say, like husband and wife. The portrait of Senenmut is even engraved in a niche in the chapel of Hathor. Senenmut was the younger brother of someone called Semnen who had been the foster-father of Queen Hatshepsut, and then of her daughter Nefrure. This position of trust passed to Senenmut, and it was responsible for some remarkable statues representing the foster-father and his ward. Statue number 2291 in the Berlin Museum is the kind of statue known as a cube statue. Senenmut is squatting, his knees up to his chin. His body is wrapped in a shroud from which the head of the royal child emerges below that of the foster-father. The Cairo Museum has another statue of Senenmut and the little girl; it was much esteemed by Legrain, who was an excellent judge of Egyptian art (Cairo 42116). Senenmut has his big hands round the slight body of the child, and his pose is full of kindness and naturalness; the child has its finger on his chin, and shows all the mischief one could wish. These statues were given by royal favour. One is tempted to wonder if some deeper bond existed between the queen and her favourite.

As an extraordinary favour, Senenmut was given permission to dig his tomb in a quarry near the great temple. At the entrance to one of the chambers there is a sketch which is hardly flattering but which is probably a good likeness of the queen's favourite.[4] One might add that the tomb remained unfinished. Senenmut was buried among the great personages of the court of Thebes. His tomb (number 71 at Gourna) is very dilapidated, but one can still admire some Egyptian bearers of offerings.

I come now to the most remarkable event in Makare's reign; its various episodes are faithfully recorded in the middle portico at Der el-Bahri. I refer to the expedition to the Terraces of Incense, or, to be more precise, to the land of Punt.[5] As we have already mentioned, the incense country had been frequented by the Egyptians at least since dynasty VI, for a sailor from Aswan records that he had been to Byblos and Punt with his masters eleven times.

Much later, under dynasty XI, Henu, a man of Coptos, reached the Red Sea and brought back fresh incense; but nothing proves that he himself went the length of the Red Sea. He could have bought his incense from a ship which was waiting for him in the Kosseir region. Other traders managed to

Senenmut, the Queen's steward and favourite, is here shown as the tutor of Princess Nefrure.

procure the precious commodity by using the Nile and the land route. But nothing is as good as direct contact, and Queen Makare was glad to establish it again when she received Amun's orders to do so, because the great god loved his daughter Makare more than all the kings who had gone before her.

The fleet which set out for the land of incense consisted of five ships and, except for a few details, they were like the ships of King Sahure ten centuries earlier. These ships were *kebenit*, that is to say they were built and launched at Byblos by Phoenicians, or perhaps built in an Egyptian shipyard like Peru-nefer, but modelled on Phoenician ships. In any case the assistance of the Phoenicians was indispensable. Probably the queen obtained it while she was negotiating a purchase of timber for Egypt from the land of Negau. Experience must have shown that the Red Sea was dangerous at the time of the

Bas-relief from the temple at Der el-Bahri, showing the chief of Punt and his obese wife receiving Hatshepsut's expedition thither.

monsoons. Perhaps the favourable season was long enough to allow the voyage there and back, but perhaps one had to allow an absence of two years.

Hugging the coast as closely as possible, the five ships finally sighted the Puntiu's houses, which were built on piles. The Puntiu had caught sight of them, and an Egyptian delegation, the Queen's messenger and a few soldiers, made contact with the Puntiu chief, Parotiu, and his wife and sons and daughter. The Puntiu were not very different from the Egyptians, but they wore long beards which, when they were plaited, looked just like the beards of Egyptian gods. The Puntian queen was enormously fat and the daughter already threatened to be very like her. The Egyptian draughtsmen, who faithfully noted the people and animals, the plants and houses, must have been struck by their silhouettes, of a type so new to them.

The god Amun-Re with Queen Hatshepsut, from one of her obelisks. She was regarded as a particular favourite of this god.

Bas-relief from Der el-Bahri : spearmen from the escort of Queen Hatshepsut's expedition to Punt.

Then the conversation began: a proof that among the visitors or the natives there was someone who understood both languages. 'How,' said the Puntiu, 'have you reached this land unknown to men? Have you come through the air? Have you journeyed by water? Have you come by land? It is Re who is sovereign of the divine land. We live by the breath he gives.' They laid a good meal in front of the Egyptians: bread, beer and wine, meat and fruit, before coming to serious matters. The incense-trees were fortunate to belong to the temple of Amun, which was their proper place, and all the good things of the divine land were put on board the ships: tree-trunks, fresh grains of incense, incense-trees wrapped up with their roots and their native soil, ebony and ivory, perfumes, and even resin from the terebinth, and pepper (which could be procured nearer home), as well as wild animals, monkeys and greyhounds.

When the ships had been loaded, they set out again for the North, and we find them assembled once more by the quay at Thebes. We have, alas, no information as to what happened in the interval. We must remember that the Egyptian artists recorded only what would serve the glory of Amun and Queen Makare. First of all, the thirty-one incense-trees were unloaded, and when their wrappings had been removed they were replanted in front of the terrace at Der el-Bahri, where archaeologists have found some of the ditches which were dug to take them. The incense grains were measured by bushels, the gold was weighed in a balance, and Thoth took notes of everything, assisted by Sesehat, the goddess of scripture.

The account preserved at Der el-Bahri ends by extolling the adventurous spirit of Queen Makare, who had explored the ways of Punt and opened the route to the Ladders of Incense. We readily join in the praise, for this expedition, which caused no deaths or casualties, was more glorious for Egypt than many inconclusive military campaigns.

This amazing expedition, and its divine origin, would have been in danger of being forgotten if the queen had not immortalised both by a monument worthy of the occasion. For its site she chose the great corrie in front of the Libyan mountain just opposite the mighty temple of Karnak, for the majesty of the place, which was dedicated to the goddess Hathor, had already attracted a certain King Mentuhotep of dynasty XI. Between this ancient monument and the rocky wall there was just room for the monument which Queen Makare intended to build. To carry out her plan the queen summoned her steward, Senenmut. Along the gently rising ground which goes up from the edge of the cultivated lands to the foot of the mountain, Senenmut built a series of three terraces. These terraces were lined with porticos, where the decorator had a great deal of room in which to evoke the glory of the reign. In order to support these porticos, Senenmut used fluted columns, capped by a mere abacus. To modern eyes they recall the simplicity of the Doric style. An avenue of sphinxes led up to the lower terrace and ended in a pair of obelisks which have now vanished.

The mortuary temple of Queen Hatshepsut in the curve of the cliffs at Der el-Bahri, opposite the site of Thebes.

Thutmose III made a savage attack on the monument. He defaced the tablets with hammers, smashed the sphinxes and buried the fragments; but the Sublime of Sublimes still remains, perhaps the most perfect monument of Egyptian art, the one in which the architect most happily adapted to its site the work he was to raise to his sovereign's glory.

(*below*) Bas-relief from the sarcophagus of Hatshepsut.

(*opposite*) Unfinished quartzite head of Queen Nefertiti, found in 1933 in the workshop of a sculptor's house at El Amarna, and now in the Cairo Museum.

Thutmose III, the warrior

When he became king Thutmose III liked to recall an incident in his child-hood. A procession which had formed behind the statue of Amun left the road it should have taken, and came towards the place where the young prince was standing; then it stopped in front of him, as if the god meant to designate his son.

Thutmose's claim to the throne was not incontestable; he was certainly the son of Thutmose II, but his mother was not of royal blood. She was a pretty woman, with wide open eyes, a delicate mouth, and a gracious expression. She remains discreetly sitting on a square seat, with her hands resting on her knees. No doubt she lacked the inordinate ambition, the spirit of intrigue, which inspired Makare. The young prince was designated to ascend the throne. He gave himself his titles, and people began to count the years of his reign, but Makare swiftly seized power, and held on to it, jealously, until her death in the year 21 or 22.

How was Thutmose treated in the interval? We have no idea. Anyhow, he lost nothing by waiting. When the way to the throne opened before him he was still very young and in full possession of his physical powers. There are many statues of Thutmose, and as they all look alike they very probably are a good representation of the original. (His nose was his dominant feature, giving character to his face. He inherited it from his father's side, as Queen Makare also had this characteristic feature.) The finest of all these statues of Thutmose was found in pieces in the favissa at Karnak, where the statue of the royal mother Isis was also found. The former has been very well restored, and we can now admire it in the Cairo Museum. The face is completely intact, and what is missing does not in the least impair the beauty of the work. It suggests a determined man whose motto might well have been what Sesostris III had said of himself: 'No sooner said than done. What my heart decides, my arm accomplishes.' The neck is short, and the chest is powerful. Thutmose was in fact a formidable man; he kept (though from time to time he modified) the titulary he had been given at the beginning:

> Horus: Valiant bull which appears at Thebes.
> Vulture-Cobra: Imposing royalty.
> Golden Horus: Magnificent in apparitions.
> King of the South and North: Menkheperre, Strong is the
> proving of Re.

Josephus put together this last name and the personal name Thutmose, making them into a composite name, Giram Mephrennethosis. Africanus and Eusebius rendered the name as Misphragamuthosis.

As we have already mentioned on page 92 the new king certainly bore no love for Queen Hatshepsut. He proved this, almost certainly at the outset of his reign. There is, however, no evidence that he took revenge on Senenmut

Detail of a limestone statue of the wife of Minnakht, a Theban nobleman. She wears a finely pleated robe and holds a necklace with a counterpoise.

and other people who had been the devoted servants of the queen (although it is probable that Senenmut died before Makare). Anyway, he had many other concerns. The princes of Djahi and Retjnu had soon noticed that Queen Makare had no aptitude for military campaigns. They saw that she preferred to embellish her noble city of Thebes (and perhaps to indulge in sweeter pastimes) and were already concentrating forces at Megiddo. They were not directly threatening Egypt, but without being a prophet one could see that they would be dangerous in the near future. Thutmose did not forget the time when a Hyksos king had been enthroned in Avaris, nor did he forget that for years the king had clung to Charohen, a city in Palestine, and he was quite determined to forestall any plans. He gathered an army together and crossed the frontier at Tjel near Pelusium, in the year 23, in the 4th month of the winter, on the 25th.[1] Nine days later he captured Giza, and continuing his march towards the North, reached the city of Yehem in the valley of the Esdradon.

There he held counsel with his valiant soldiers and expressed himself as follows:

The vile fallen man of Kadesh is come. He has entered Megiddo, where he now abides, he has gathered round him the leaders of every land who were in the waters of Egypt, as well as the Nahrin, the Syrians, the Kode, their horses, their soldiers and all their men. I am told that he said: 'I am waiting to fight here at Megiddo'. Tell me what you think.

(At this point I must open parentheses. War was not a confused *mêlée* of two conflicting armies, hurling themselves against one another. It was waged according to certain laws, and these laws were in the safe keeping of the gods. In an old text of the Middle Kingdom the Aamu were even reproached for not announcing the day of the battle. Since then, through their contact with the Egyptians, they had changed their customs. The events which we now relate had been preceded by an exchange of missives. When the 'vile fallen man' announced that he was waiting at Megiddo, he asked Thutmose to name the day when he expected to attack, and implicitly engaged not to make a surprise attack on him.)

There were three possible routes from Yehem to Megiddo. The most direct road soon became so narrow that they would have had to march in single file, horse behind horse, man behind man, so that the vanguard could be engaged in combat while the rearguard was still peacefully at Aruna. There were two other routes: one ended at Taanach, west of Megiddo; the second reached the causeways north of Djefti and north of Megiddo. Thutmose's soldiers answered him: 'May our valiant lord, in the excellence of his heart, make us march down those paths upon the fallen men. Do not make us march along these difficult paths.' (A phrase which has been partly obliterated seems to indicate that the enemy had suggested it.) The king replied:

Kneeling, the pharaoh Thutmose III, offers sacrifices to Amun-Re.

I live. Re loves me. My father Amun praises me. My nose flourishes in life and length of days.

My Majesty will take the Aruna road. He who wants may take the road you speak of. He who wants may follow My Majesty. What would these fallen men think, these men whom God holds in horror? 'His Majesty is taking another road. He is going away for fear of us.' That is what they would think.

The soldiers answered His Majesty: 'Your father Amun will do according to your will. As for us, we are in Your Majesty's service, wherever Your Majesty may be. The servant will follow his Master.' At this His Majesty swore a great oath and said: 'I shall not make my valiant soldiers march before My Majesty', and decided to march himself at the head of his soldiers.

On the 19th of the first month of summer, a council was held in His Majesty's tent in the village of Aruna. Thutmose wanted to go on towards the North under the protection of his father Amun, 'the opener of paths'. The south wing of his army was at Taanach and the north wing at the bend (south of the valley of Kina). And this is what they said to His Majesty, Life, Health, Strength: 'Behold, Your Majesty appears with his best soldiers, who have taken the valley. This time may our Master obey. May our Master allow us to wait for the rearguard of his troops.' The king granted this wish. He reached the bank of the Kina canal south of Megiddo by the seventh hour of the day. The canal was crossed, and the soldiers were given their instructions. 'Attention . . . Prepare your weapons. For in the morning we shall fight the vile fallen man.' There was a great inspection of weapons, and one cannot refrain from noting that the 'vile fallen man' kept scrupulously to his promise. There were many occasions on which he could have caused alarm and dismay among the Egyptians, but he waited until it had made its arrangements to fight with equal weapons.

On the morning of the 21st of the first month of summer, the feast day of the Enneade, the king rose and set himself at the head of his troops. He went forth in his golden chariot, equipped with all his weapons, like Horus and Monthu. His father Amun had given strength to his arms. The south wing had the mountain south of Kina as its objective. The right wing had the north-west of Megiddo, and His Majesty had the centre. The engagement was short. The enemy abandoned their horses and chariots and rushed to shut themselves up in Megiddo. 'If it had pleased heaven that His Majesty's soldiers should not have stopped to pillage these fallen men, they would have taken Megiddo instantly.' The Egyptians collected some splendid booty but they had to resign themselves to a siege which lasted seven months.

At the end of these seven months, the leaders of the country dragged themselves, prostrate, to His Majesty, and kissed the ground before His Majesty's people, and implored breath for their nostrils. They delivered up gold and silver, lapis and turquoise, and fresh victuals for the troops. As the Egyptians had taken all the horses the prince of Megiddo's allies were compelled to ride home on asses. The Egyptian scribe who noted this detail must have done so with a certain malice.

It was a hard lesson for the Syrians, but nothing is ever ended in the East, and Thutmose was to find the same enemies, and others, either in the Djahi, or in northern Syria and on the Euphrates, or in the lands of the South, at least until the year 42.

In the year 29 he ravaged the Djahi and captured two enemy ships. In the year 30 he destroyed Kadesh on the Orontes, and reached Simyra on the coast. The following year he conquered Tunip, and the great army of the Mitanni was annihilated in an hour. The Egyptians crossed the Euphrates at Carchemish in boats made of pinewood from the land of Megau, a dependency of Byblos; the boats had been dragged by oxen from the banks of the Orontes to the Euphrates. His Majesty did not stay north of the great river for long, returning to Niy where the water flowed between two rocks. It was there that he encountered a troop of elephants, an excellent occasion to procure the rare and beautiful ivory. The biggest elephant approached, and the king was in great danger, but an experienced officer cut off the elephant's trunk before it reached him. The king briefly mentions this incident, but he does not record the officer Amenemhab's devotion. It would have been forgotten if the brave man had not recorded it himself. The same Amenemhab distinguished himself again in the operations against the prince of Kadesh. The prince had let loose a mare on heat, and she rushed among the soldiers, Amenemhab ran with his sword, slit her belly open, cut off her tail and presented it to the king.[2] It seems in character that he was the first warrior to enter Kadesh.

It needs a miracle to sanction so many victories, so many deeds of renown. Two guards on duty observed a star which shot across the heavens from north to south. This phenomenon did not surprise the Egyptians, but it completely demoralised their enemies, and their horses galloped no more.

The enormous booty captured by the Egyptians throughout Syria was sent in Cretan ships to the ports which the pharaoh had taken; pinewood giblites and *skwt* were laden with thick planks, beams, and massive lengths of timber for His Majesty's great shipyards. The ports were also provisioned with every sort of merchandise.[3]

These extremely fruitful campaigns did not distract the attention of the king from the southern lands. Until now the Egyptians had hardly gone beyond the Second Cataract. It was perhaps under Thutmose III that they reached the sacred mountain: the Gebel Barkal, a little way downstream from the Fourth Cataract. It was here that Reisner found the magnificent stele on which the king's exploits in Syria are recounted in detail.

It was even more important to make them known to the Thebans: to thank the gods and edify the populace. Passing the sixth pylon in the centre of the great temple of Amun, one finds oneself in a quite compact building; here everywhere one looks one sees the names of the warrior king.[4] Here he is seen overwhelming his enemies; there he is taking an enormous booty from Syria, and objects which have been made in Theban workrooms from the products of his campaigns. The cities of the southern lands are like those of the north: each of them is inscribed in a crenellated oval, in which appears a figure representing the land in question. The annals are complete.

Beyond the ruins of the temple of the Middle Kingdom we find the building called Menkheperre Akh-menu, 'Menkheperre is glorious with memories', which some consider a room for festive occasions. It is in fact a long portico, and its columns are perhaps the one unsuccessful creation of Egyptian art. In a corner of this building was the list of the ancestral kings which Prisse d'Avesne carried off in sections to the Louvre. This building also contains what is called the botanical garden, but only an inadequate record is left.[5] Did Thutmose III want to vie with Queen Makare, who had had the incense trees from Punt replanted at Der el-Bahri? Among the birds and antelopes we can recognise irises, chrysanthemums and pomegranate trees, which the Egyptian draughtsman has not reproduced with his usual diligence.

Nothing could be more striking, on the other hand, than the many obelisks erected at Karnak and Heliopolis. Their tops were covered with golden cowls, and sometimes as much as a third of the obelisk would be covered in gold. During the day they shone with the fires of the sun and at night under the moon they cast a mysterious light. Two of these obelisks are now separated by the Atlantic, in London and Washington, a third is at Istanbul. The texts also mention two pairs of obelisks, of which the exact situation is unknown. The one that is best constructed is the single obelisk, the highest of them all, ninety-six feet high; it was originally erected in the courtyard of the temple near Ipet-Esut (Karnak).

Thutmose proclaimed his gratitude and that of the goddess of Thebes on a granite stela which was engraved with remarkable care. As it happens, this noble monument has been very little damaged. On most stelae the king addresses the god, but here the god himself recalls how he was pleased to guide the king. Then, carried away by his theme and by his inspiration, the god begins to speak in verse.[6]

I

I came. I let you trample down the great men of Djahi.
I spread them out beneath your feet all along their mountains.
I let them see Your Majesty as a master of sunrays.
You blazed out in their face like my image.

II

I came. I let you trample down those who are in Asia.
Thou shalt break the heads of the Aamu of Retjnu.
I let them see Your Majesty adorned with your ornaments
When you received the weapons of war on your chariot.

The tops of the obelisks of Hatshepsut and Thutmose I, in the Temple of Amun at Karnak, were originally gilded.

III

I came. I let you trample down the Land of the East.
You crushed those who dwelt in the cantons of the Divine Land.
I let them see Your Majesty as a meteor which
Flashes light and gives rain.

IV

I came. I let you trample down the Land of the West.
Keftiu and Cyprus are in terror of you.
I let them see Your Majesty as a young and ardent bull
With sharp horns.

V

I came. I let you trample down those who were in their ships.
The lands of Mitanni trembled with the fear of you.
I let them see Your Majesty, master of fear in the midst of the water.
They came not near.

VI

I came. I let you trample down those who were in the isles
In the midst of the most green under your war cries.
I let them see Your Majesty as the avenger who appears
On the back of his capture.

VII

I came. I let you trample down the Tjehnyu.
The isles of the Utentiu belonged to the power of your Souls.
I let them see Your Majesty as a lion.
You made corpses of them along their valleys.

VIII

I came. I let you trample down the far corners of the lands.
The circle of the Ocean was caught in your fist.
I let them see Your Majesty as a master of wings
Taking in a glance what he wants.

IX

I came. I let you trample down those who are in [———]
You made the Nomads prisoners.
I let him see Your Majesty as the jackal of the South, master of the [———],
Swift when he crosses the two lands.

X

I came. I let you crush the Troglodytes of Nubia
As far as the land of Chah in your fist.
I let them see Your Majesty like your two brothers.
For you I united the strength of their arms.

In spite of some clumsy expressions, due to a limited vocabulary, the piece has a certain style. One would like to know the author: it might easily be the king himself. Kamose handled invective like a master. Why should not Thutmose have been inspired with lyricism?

His general survey begins with the Djahi and Syria. He goes from the East to the West, devotes two verses to the seafaring peoples and the rest of the poem to the inhabitants of Africa, even the most distant among them. Each verse is divided into two parts. The vanquished people are named, and then the pharaoh appears to them in the guise most likely to frighten them: sometimes, as in Crete and Cyprus, he appears in the likeness of their own god, a young bull with sharp horns. The reader will have noticed that Thutmose showed an equal disdain for the inhabitants of the countries which had actually been conquered as for others – the Hellenes, Cretans and Cypriots – who had never, as far as one knows, seen the invader.

New Year's Day in Egypt fell at the beginning of the floods; it was – as it is with us – a moment for the exchange of presents and good wishes. Pharaoh received good wishes and distributed the gifts which had been prepared during the past year in the royal workrooms. The gifts were laid out in a vast room in the palace, in which a canopy had been set up with two chairs for the king and queen. The chief of works and his principal assistants would greet their sovereigns, and present them with some masterpieces of workmanship. Then the king and queen would come down from the platform and tour the exhibition, where naturally the king showed particular interest in the weapons, and the queen in the articles of finery. A scribe took note of the statues and precious vases which were to be despatched to foreign princes. So it was that some alabaster vases, engraved with the names of Thutmose III, were recently discovered in Candia.[7]

An alabaster vase, perhaps sent as a gift to a foreign ruler.

(*above*) Thutmose III standing before a
god carved on a fallen section of his
temple wall at Karnak.

(*opposite*) The uraeus, clearly seen on
this head of Thutmose III, was used as a
symbol of royal rank.

The reception of the foreign ambassadors with their bearers of offerings was the occasion for showing a splendour which was worthy of Egypt. The ceremony took place in a vast courtyard where a double canopy, decorated with great magnificence, had been set up over a dais. The king seated himself on his throne before which the heaviest gifts had already been deposited. Each delegation was presented by a high Egyptian dignitary. The foreign envoys prostrated themselves, recited a petition or a compliment which the king heard impassively, and offered him a valuable gift. The vizier Rekhmire once decided to present four diplomatic processions on a single occasion: they had come from the four corners of the horizon, and there was a fifth procession of hostages. Perhaps this was just a trick of composition, allowing the artist to combine different episodes in one picture. But there is no reason why things should not have happened like this, and why the king should not have received the five processions at one audience.

The people from Punt were presented first, which was just. The Puntiu had always given the Egyptians a good reception, ever since that day in Makare's reign when the expedition had been greeted by the strange queen with quivering flesh. 'They come in peace, the leaders of Punt, bowing, with their heads bent under their gifts. They come wherever he is found, His Majesty Menkheperre living for ever; they bring every good offering from their land, the land which no one else had visited . . . Now all lands are His Majesty's inheritance . . .' The Puntiu did not only bring various forms of incense, but skins and tails, tusks and feathers, wooden weapons and live animals, giraffes, monkeys and baboons. (It is not known whether Thutmose III repeated Queen Makare's exploit and sent his fleets to the villages, built on piles, where the Puntiu lived, but we cannot exclude this. We must remember that there was more than one route for bringing the products of Punt to Egypt: there was the Nile, and there was the land route, and ships hugged the coast from one place of call to the next.)

The inhabitants of the Keftiu and the islands of the sea had not really been conquered. No doubt the Egyptians had requisitioned their ships as they lay at anchor in the ports of the Djahi, to carry their plunder back to Egypt; and the owners of the ships would have been forced to bear their misfortune with good grace if they were ever to get them back. The inhabitants of the Keftiu were popular in Egypt, with their long ringlets, their rhytons and goblets. They had already been seen in the days of Senenmut and Makare and were often to reappear under Thutmose III and his immediate successors, that is, under the most powerful pharaohs. After that no more was heard of them.

On registers 3 and 4, made on this occasion, are listed the southerners and the people of Retjnu: the peoples who for centuries had been liable to taxation and statute-labour. There is a final fifth register filled with the children of the princes of these peoples.

The audience has come to an end. The raw materials and the finished

The face of a yellow-skinned and bearded man represented both a foreigner and the hieroglyph 'Hr'.

Scenes from the Asiatic campaigns of Thutmose III, carved on the walls of Amun's temple at Karnak. Here he is shown smiting the Asiatics.

Captives kneeling in supplication before the conquering pharaoh.

articles are all collected together in the pharaoh's storerooms and workrooms, and the best possible use is made of them.

There were other occasions, too, for the king to show himself in public. When he had decided to reward his most faithful servants, he appeared on the balcony which was designed for royal appearances. The royal herald summoned the elect, and they were presented to the pharaoh. They had to catch a golden bowl and a golden cup which – with a noble gesture – His Majesty tossed them. The Louvre has a cup which King Menkheperre gave to the noble prince the heavenly father, who 'filled the king's heart through all the lands and the islands of the sea'. It was the king's duty to be generous to his servants. When Thutmose was leading one of his victorious campaigns, he never strayed very far from his troops, and as soon as the royal herald signalled some remarkable deed, he would take a valuable gift from a coffer to present it to the brave warrior.

Thutmose III was extremely brave in war and readily exposed himself to danger; he was also a pious king. At Karnak there are countless proofs of this piety. He shows it chiefly to Amun, but he does not neglect his ancestors, and in the Akh-menu building he had engraved the names of sixty-one kings, beginning with Snofru the Beneficent, and presented in an order which has caused much trouble among historians. One of the first acts of his reign was to restore the statues of Amenhotep I and Thutmose II. At Sinai he restored an ancient inscription of Sesostris III, a king with whom he felt he had affinities.

Apart from the Theban family, the goddess Hathor, of many aspects, was the one who inspired the pharaoh with the liveliest devotion. She might appear as a woman with a cow's head, or with a human head but wearing the disc with horns round it, or she might even appear as a cow, pushing aside two tufts of papyrus with its muzzle in order to present itself to its worshippers. It was evidently as a cow that she appeared to Thutmose, when he was visiting the left bank of the Nile – perhaps to choose the site for his funerary temple. At once he rushed to the goddess's udders and began to drink her milk. Having drunk he himself became divine, and that is why the creator of the admirable monument at Der el-Bahri painted his flesh black, as was generally done with a certain Queen Nofretari and also with the wooden statues which guarded the entrance to Tutankhamun's tomb.[8]

Thutmose certainly had a number of wives and concubines. Three of them were accorded the honour of figuring with the king in a chamber of his tomb: Queen Meryetre, who was still alive, and Queen Satyah and Queen Nebetu, who with one of his daughters, Neferiru, were dead. In the chamber of his tomb, Thutmose is shown approaching the sacred tree where his own mother Isis is disguised as the goddess Nut. She has given him her breast and the king has seized it as avidly as if he were still an infant.[9]

The king's favourite wife was probably Meryetre, for it was she who gave him the hereditary prince Amenhotep. Mother and son are sometimes shown

Akhenaten, his wife and two daughters hold flowers in worship towards the Aten or sun disc.

side by side, and we know that Thutmose watched most attentively over his son's education – his education as a sportsman that is. He gave him a prince of This and of the Oasis to teach him archery, and under such a master the young man made rapid progress, soon becoming the equal of his father.

He bent three hundred bows to compare the work of the different makers, so that he could distinguish the ignorant artisan from the expert. He even went so far as to do what I am about to relate. Behold, he entered his northern stand and found the four targets of Asian copper, a palm in thickness, which had been set up at intervals of five cubits.

When His Majesty appeared on his stand, like Montu in his strength, he seized his bow, grasped four arrows at once, and went forward, shooting at the targets.

Each arrow in turn went through the target and His Majesty shot at the next one.

In the art of breaking horses, the young prince was soon unrivalled. 'This was heard in the royal palace by his father, the powerful Horus falcon rising in Thebes. The heart of His Majesty was content, and he rejoiced in what was said of his eldest son.' The young prince had, of course, an example before him. Thutmose himself was so fond of horses that he had set up a magnificent stable (and as we have seen, he had kept all the horses belonging to the prince of Megiddo's allies, compelling them to ride home on asses). Now Thutmose gave orders: 'Give my son a perfect team of horses from My Majesty's stable at Memphis. Tell him to take care of them, make them obedient, make them trot, look after them.' The prince duly chose a team of horses from the royal stable and trained them into horses beyond compare. They seemed to be tireless as long as he held the reins. Even in a long race, they did not sweat.[10] So Thutmose taught his son to scorn physical softness, and to appreciate toughness. Just as he had once prepared himself for his royal duties, so he now prepared his heir.

Thutmose was a tough warrior who could not have been much moved by the sight of bloodshed; one is glad to find that he had human feelings. He loved and venerated his mother, and no doubt loved the mother of the hereditary prince. The exploits of this prince, this complete athlete, this oarsman, archer and horseman, filled him with vast pride and reassured him about the future of his dynasty. For his companions-in-arms, who had more than once saved his life, Thutmose may have known a feeling akin to friendship. Incidentally, it is Amenemhab, one of these companions-in-arms, who has revealed the exact length of his reign: 'Now the king had accomplished his length of days in many noble years, in valiance, in strength, in triumph, from the Year I to the Year LIV, the third month of the winter, the last day.'[11] From these fifty-four years we must subtract – which the old soldier neglected to do – the twenty-odd years during which Makare-Hatshepsut reigned alone. That still makes a reign of more than thirty years; and of this one may say, with Amenemhab, that it was well spent.

The hypostyle of Amun-Re's temple at Karnak had columns over nine yards in circumference to support the roof.

The kings of the Old and Middle Kingdoms liked to build their temple for their funerary cult next to their pyramid. It was on the left bank of the Nile, at the foot of the Kuru mountain, that the sovereigns of the New Kingdom scattered their temples, in which men would honour the gods of Thebes and the royal memory. As for the tombs, they were dug in the valley of the Kuru mountain (Biban el-Moluk), which was considered a sort of communal pyramid. The temple of Thutmose was demolished almost to its foundations. His tomb was found in a narrow passage, less than three feet wide, some thirty feet below the soil. V. Loret was its first visitor. He found the ground suddenly collapsing under his feet and as he hurriedly came up from the well he reached a chamber cluttered with debris, and then another chamber, the sarcophagus chamber. The walls were decorated with figures in outline and cursive hieroglyphics in black and red on an ochre background; it was as if they were hung with some papyrus which had been gigantically enlarged. The sarcophagus was empty, and one could not expect to find the royal mummy: it had been on show at the Giza Museum for some fifteen years.

During the time of the last of the Ramses the Egyptians had stopped obeying their kings and priests; indeed the priests became the worst offenders. They used to guide armed bands to the treasures of the temples and to the chambers of the tombs where the pharaohs and princes lay covered with gold and jewels. The first thieves were not heavily punished. This encouraged general lawlessness, and soon no tomb – or hardly any tomb – remained intact. This anarchy lasted several years, perhaps several decades, stopping only when there was nothing else to steal. The government appointed commissions and started enquiries. The violated tombs could not be completely restored, but the kings' mummies could be taken to a burial-place where nobody would disturb their rest. In the rocky wall between the corrie of Der el-Bahri and the next corrie, they found the place they had been looking for. All the coffins they had managed to save were placed there, at the end of a long corridor, piled up in no particular order. In two days of unremitting

The horned viper was used as a hieroglyph to represent the sound 'f'.

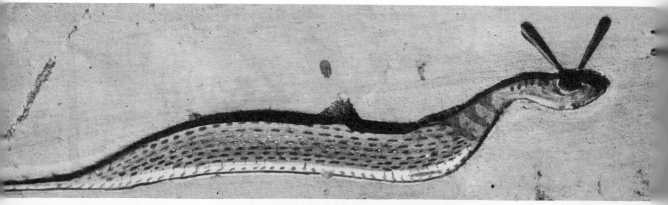

labour by modern archaeologists, everything was exhumed, and the freight crossed the plain of Thebes to the place where the museum steamer was waiting. It was escorted by all the inhabitants of the river banks, men and women, shouting and firing shots.

Thutmose III was not particularly favoured during these journeyings. His mummy, stripped of all ornaments, was laid in a modest coffin of gilded wood, a coffin which had already been used for somebody else. The mummy was in a deplorable state, and measured 4 foot 6 inches only after several repairs.

And that was all that remained of the king who had made the Orient tremble.

Portrait head of Thutmose III that closely resembles his mummy.

Head of Amenhotep III, showing the stylisation and slight abstraction of the art of this reign. The pharaoh appears more as a god than a conqueror.

Amenhotep III, the magnificent

Thutmose III was followed by two kings who, like himself, preferred the works of Monthu to those of Thoth. The second, however, Thutmose IV, allowed himself a luxury: he completed a work which his ancestor's engineers had left unfinished. When they had brought the single obelisk, the tallest known, to its site, they had been obliged to abandon the idea of erecting it on its base. The engineers of Thutmose IV performed this remarkable feat.[1]

When Thutmose IV died in 1408, he was succeeded by his son, Amenhotep III. Amenhotep took as his solar name Nebmare, 'Re is the master of truth'; it has more than once been transcribed as Nimmuaria on the cuneiform tablets of El-Amarna. Amenhotep's mother was called Mutemuia, 'Mut is in the solar barge'. On the bas-reliefs of the temple at Luxor she looks like her husband. Amun did for Mutemuia what he had once done for Queen Ahmose, wife of Thutmose I. We know very little about Mutemuia. The British Museum has a model of the solar barge in black granite, but the queen is broken at the waist. A statue was found at Dendera, but it is hardly more satisfactory. We should be sceptical about the theory that Mutemuia is a Mitannian princess, King Artatama's daughter, and that Thutmose IV had demanded her and finally obtained her for his harem. Towards the middle of dynasty XVIII, the pharaohs readily took their womenfolk from neighbouring countries. But there is no record that Mutemuia from Mitanni took or received an Egyptian name when she came to Thebes. To put it briefly, Amenhotep III is the son of Thutmose IV and the royal wife Mutemuia, of whom we know only the name and a few titles.

The British Museum has an admirable head of Amenhotep III. The sculptor has given the king the typical southern Egyptian features: a long, slightly *retroussé* nose, the eyes turned up towards the temples, and something of a nutcracker chin. The two Leningrad sphinxes are very similar to this, but the expression is younger. One often finds good examples of the identical type round Thebes today. A modern sculptor who took them as models would come very close to Amenhotep III.

Manetho's abbreviators sometimes give Amenhotep thirty years, sometimes thirty-four. This last figure is nearer the truth, for the year 37 had begun when he died.

The reign of Amenhotep III presents two important new features. When the king received news which he considered vital and interesting, he announced it by issuing scarabs to his court and to the people of Thebes. So it was that a scarab – of which there were many copies – certified that between the year 1 and the year 10, Amenhotep himself killed one hundred and two lions. After the year 10, he seems to have tired of this dangerous pastime.[2] But another scarab announces the king's marriage to Tiye.

Warlike activity was much reduced, diplomatic activity was intense. The

The solar barge of Queen Mutemuia, mother of Amenhotep III.

missives which the pharaoh exchanged with mighty and lesser kings were drawn up in Babylonian and transcribed in cuneiform. A body of interpreters at the court of Thebes translated the tablets as they arrived and drew up the replies. It is beyond the scope of this work to study the political situation in the ancient world but as an example of a missive I will quote a letter from Rib-Addi, king of Byblos, asking for help against the Amorrheens. The kings of Byblos could use hieroglyphics, but in this case they wrote like the other Asiatic kings:

Rib-Addi to the king my lord:
I have cast myself under the feet of my lord seven times and again seven times. Behold, I have heard the words of the king my lord and my heart has greatly rejoiced in them. Let my lord swiftly hasten the sending of troops. If the king my lord does not send troops, we die, and the city of Gubla is taken . . . Behold, I myself guard the city

Scarab issued by Amenhotep III to commemorate his marriage to Queen Tiye.

of Gubla by night and by day . . . Many leaders do not like troops to set out when things are going well for them. But I myself want them to set out because things are going ill for me. Let the king my lord set out on his way, let him see his country and take possession of everything. Behold, the day you set out on your way, all the land will rally to the king my lord. Who can resist the soldiers of the king? . . .[3]

It is very unlikely that the king troubled to go in person. A patrol and a little gold were enough to reassure Rib-Addi, and timber from the Lebanon was sent to Egypt as usual.

In the year 10, Amenhotep III had begun negotiations with Shuttarna, king of Nahrin. When the king's daughter arrived in Egypt, Amenhotep issued scarabs which read: 'A marvel happened to His Majesty, Life, Health, Strength, when Kirgipa, the daughter of the king of Nahrin Shuttarna, arrived with three hundred and seventeen ladies-in-waiting.'[4]

Relations with the king of Babylon had become more confident. However, when Amenhotep demanded a Babylonian woman for his harem, he refused to send an Egyptian woman in return. The two sovereigns contented themselves with exchanging gifts. Amenhotep III then turned to the Mitanni once again, sending their king an ambassador extraordinary by the name of Mani, with presents and a letter: 'The gifts that I send are nothing, but if you grant me the woman I want, the presents will come.' The king of Mitanni did not wish to offend his brother. He presented his daughter Tadukhipa to Mani, and Mani saw her and greatly rejoiced in her. The princess left escorted by the ambassador with a household composed of several hundred women, a chapel, and a healing statue. The king of Mitanni, for his part, expected to receive a good deal of gold.[5]

We have no idea at all how Amenhotep III behaved to these noble foreign princesses. It is certain, however, that an Egyptian woman, the daughter of noble parents, was the great royal wife at the beginning of the reign (the year is not specified), and that after her marriage it was she who took part in all the royal ceremonies. She survived her husband and we shall meet her again in the following chapter. The scarab called the Marriage scarab – at least twelve copies of it still exist – gives us her name, Tiye. It also gives us the name of her father, the divine father of the master of the two lands, Yuia, and the name of her mother, Tjuia. Both parents bear titles which relate them to the god Min of Panopolis in the tenth nome of Upper Egypt.[6] Perhaps this is why the king gave the queen a fine estate called Dja-ukha (seeker of the night), not far from Panopolis.[7] A little upstream from Soleb he also built a temple called the court of Tiye, which may well have been Tiye's birthplace.

The king did a quite exceptional favour for his parents-in-law: he reserved them a small chamber in the Valley of Kings. Theodore Davis discovered it in 1905. The thieves had clearly discovered it many years earlier, and had stripped the mummies of their ornaments, but they had left the funerary furniture. Until the discovery of Tutankhamun's tomb, it was the finest known collection of such furniture, with its two vegetating Osiris, its votive chariot and its three armchairs – one of which is often pointed out as the Empire chair. Princess Sitamun had given this furniture to her grandparents.

One must admit that the great royal wife, Tiye, was not very beautiful or even very gracious. A head was found in the Sinai peninsula which is now exhibited in the Cairo Museum; it is authenticated by the inscription engraved in the middle of the crown. The nose is broad, the nostrils disdainful, the mouth heavy and sullen, and the lower lip is drawn back by a retreating chin. The eyes turn up towards the temples. These features, not in the least attenuated, indeed carried to the verge of caricature, are found again on a head in the Berlin Museum. But Queen Tiye must have had considerable influence on her husband. She is shown beside him on the colossi at Memnon, and again on a gigantic group in the Cairo Museum. The latter was found in the temple dedicated to the cult of the king and to that of the god of the Theban plain; but it is a conventional work, and rather heavy, adding nothing to our knowledge of the king and queen.

The king's taste for splendid buildings was much encouraged by a number of architects, the best that Egypt had known since the days of Sesostris. First among them we must mention a man of Athribis in Lower Egypt, called Amenhotpe, a name similar to his sovereign. In order not to be confused with the many Amenhotpe, he had also taken his father's name, Hapu, and, as that was not enough, a surname, Huy.[8] The favissa at Karnak has given us a statue of this accomplished architect at the age of eighty, and it is one of the masterpieces of Egyptian sculpture. The old man has clearly preserved his intellectual faculties and almost all his physical vigour. He does not seem to want to disguise the fact that he hopes to reach the age of a hundred and ten, which the Egyptians considered to be the natural span of human life. He was much attached to his local god and to the Theban triad, and he kept the royal favour until his last breath. The king let him build a funerary temple behind his own temple, and made a royal decree to ensure the permanent cult of the great man.[9] The decree has been either destroyed or was lost, but we have a copy, made in dynasty XXI; the temple was still standing in the Ptolemaic period. The great architect's reputation as a scholar, sage and magician had only grown with time. It has even been claimed that Amenhotep III, who wanted to see the god, had confided this desire to him, and that Amenhotpe, son of Hapu, had suggested that he rid Egypt of the people who were known as the Impure. But there we are no longer in the realm of history.

After Amenhotpe, son of Hapu, we must mention the twin brothers, Suti and Hor, who played an important part in the building of Karnak and Luxor. They speak with one voice:

I am chief in your Apit and director of works at one of the official sanctuaries which Nebmare, your beloved son, built for you. My master knows I am vigilant, and he has entrusted me with the supervision of your monuments. I have been an energetic chief where your monuments were concerned. You make me great, for I have known Maat on earth, and as I have known him, so you have made me great. You grant me favours in Karnak, for I am in your procession when you show yourself in public . . . My brother, my twin, came from the womb at the same time as I did in these fortunate days. . . . I am chief in the West, and he is chief in the East. We are directing the building of great monuments in Apit south of Thebes, the city of Amun.

The celebration of the royal jubilee was a time of festivities, and it was also a duty which the king could not avoid, as it was traditionally an occasion when the royal family mingled with the people. Amenhotep III celebrated his first jubilee in the year 30; he celebrated his second six years later, almost on the eve of his death. The episodes of this second jubilee are recounted at Soleb and in the king's other sanctuaries. We also find an entertaining record in the tomb of Kheruef, a high dignitary of the queen's. The king and queen and the

Vestibule of the temple of Amenhotep III at Luxor, dedicated to Amun, Mut and Chons. The names of the gods were defaced on Akhenaten's orders.

princesses left the palace and made their way to a richly decorated canopy. On the morning of the jubilee they duly raised the *djed* (this looks like a pillar with the upper part crossed by horizontal bars), having summoned women from the oasis to help them. The pillar is hung with raiment and insignia, and offerings are made to it. Then the king mounted the steps to the canopy, and, in memory of the time when Egypt was composed of two kingdoms, has himself crowned with the crown of the South, then with the crown of the North. This was the moment for the crowd of spectators to relax. Singers and musicians excited the scantily dressed dancing women. The men divided into two groups, those of Pe and Dep, which were two neighbouring cities in the Delta; they fought each other, and prided themselves that they had even caught the Horus Khaemhat, the king himself. The celebrations might continue for several days. Oxen were slain. There was eating and drinking. The dances went on more wildly than ever, and only came to an end when the dancers were physically exhausted. No doubt the king and queen had long since returned to their apartments, for in the year 30 and particularly in the year 36, they were too old for revelry like this; but the people must have been glad to have looked upon their masters.

It is now time for us to visit the principal buildings which Amenhotep III, and his great architects, had erected along the Nile. Between the Third and Second Cataracts, at the place we now call Soleb, Amenhotep III had built the castle of Khaemhat. The building was artistically as perfect as the most elaborate monuments of Thebes. It was heralded by an avenue of crouching rams, lions and falcons. In the British Museum we can admire

(*opposite*) Between the paws of each ram stood the figure of a god or pharaoh.

(*below*) The statues of rams erected by Amenhotep III in the first court of the temple at Karnak, on the right bank of the Nile.

a pair of lions with crossed paws and their heads turned to one side; they were carried off by Tutankhamun and transported further south, to Gebel Barkal. Then came the features which were common to most Egyptian temples: the pylon, a courtyard with porticos round the sides, and two hypostyle rooms, carved and sculpted as carefully as the ones in the temple at Luxor.

When it was time to consecrate the buildings, the king came in person, accompanied by the indispensable Queen Tiye and by his favourite architect, Amenhotpe, the man most versed in knowledge of the rites. The king struck the door of the first room twelve times with his white stone mace, then the door of the Holy of Holies; finally he entered and installed his own statue and all the other statues which made up the local Enneade. There was a great procession and endless recitations until finally, they returned to the palace for a great banquet.

Before these events took place, some official had duly examined the lists of the southern peoples. On these lists, which were inscribed on stone, every race was represented by a native figure who emerged from the oval bearing his name. One of these figures (which are of special interest to scholars) bears the name of Punt of Asia. Until now Punt had been considered an exclusively African country. In fact it stretched down both banks of the strait of Bab el-Mandeb, and the Asiatic bank also furnished incense and perfumes.

As we re-enter Egypt, we shall pause briefly at the isle of Elephantine. It was here that Amenhotep III built a delightful oratory for the god of the cataract and his two consorts, Anukhit and Satis. It was destroyed in 1822, and we should not know of it if it had not been drawn and described by the Bonaparte Commission. It is as delicate and graceful as the White Chapel of Sesostris I, and both buildings recall the perfection of the Greek temple.

We arrive now in the city of a hundred gates, the city which owes to Amenhotep III much of its splendour. At Karnak, he completely rebuilt the sanctuary of Mut, and also enlarged the Sacred Lake; in the temple courtyard he assembled hundreds of statues of Sekhmet, the goddess with the lion's head, which he identified with Amun's *paredre*.

At Luxor he had the traces of the Middle Kingdom removed, in their place erecting one of the most successful buildings in Egypt. We need not concern ourselves here with the pylon, the obelisks, and the first courtyard, for they are the work of Ramses II. In the days of dynasty XVIII one entered a vestibule, formed by giant pillars with palmiform capitals, leading to the huge courtyard with bunched columns; from this one entered the hypostyle room and the Holy of Holies. The temple of Luxor served a dual purpose. It was here that the Theban triad was worshipped. Also, during the great feast of the middle of the flood, the three great barges of Amun, Mut and Chons remained at anchor there for several days. An avenue of crouching rams led out towards the north, reaching towards the gates of old Thebes.

(*opposite*) Black granite statue of Amenhotpe, son of Hapu, Master of Works, from Karnak. In reward for the building of the temple at Luxor and other works, he was granted the unprecedented honour of a funerary temple in his lifetime.

The temple which Amenhotep raised to himself and Amun on the west bank of the Nile almost completely eclipsed the work of his predecessors, for the vast mud-brick enclosure, of which fragments have been found, measured about five hundred by six hundred yards.

As for the sumptuous temple inside, a strange caprice of nature and human-kind has preserved the two colossi seated in front of the pylon. To Roman travellers they were one of the curiosities of Thebes. Legend had claimed them as its own since it had been discovered that the southern colossus uttered a sound at sunrise. This colossus has been identified with Memnon, son of Aurora, but to Egyptians the colossi represented their old king, Amenhotep III, with two feminine effigies: the royal mother Mutemuia and the royal wife Tiye. The great hieroglyphics of the dorsal pillar summarise the history of the monument.

To begin with, Amenhotep's titles recall these claims to glory:

Valiant bull, prince of princes, most glorious within Thebes: Nebmare Amenhotep, Vulture-Cobra, great with monuments in Thebes brought from Heliopolis in the North to Heliopolis in the South, beloved of Sokar.
Golden Horus who has enlarged his temple for ever.
He has made a statue of himself for his father Amun, a great statue of sandstone called: Nebmare is the sovereign of sovereigns.

We have additional information from Amenhotpe, son of Hapu, who directed all the sculpting and the transport of the colossi.

The king [said the great architect] appointed me chief of works in the red mountain, not far from Heliopolis, where sandstone has been dug at least since the Middle Kingdom. He commanded me to direct the execution of the monuments dedicated to his father Amun of Karnak. I had mighty monuments transported, statues of His Majesty contrived with skilful art. They were brought from Heliopolis in the North to Heliopolis in the South, and they are to be found on the eastern bank.

In fact the sandstone quarries are not exactly at Heliopolis in the North, and the temple of the colossi stands at an appreciable distance from Erment (Heliopolis in the South); but Amenhotpe, no doubt, wanted to associate two such illustrious names in one inscription.

Other statues have been discovered behind the colossi in the temple's enclosure: the enormous group in the Cairo Museum, the two sphinxes now in Leningrad, and some stelae. However precious these relics may be, they are only an infinitesimal fraction of the contents of one of the most prodigious monuments ever raised by a pharaoh.

There was probably a royal residence there, as there was at Ramesseum and Medinet Habu. Amenhotep III seems to have liked the left bank of the Nile; a little further south he also reserved for himself a vast tract of land on which he built a palace called 'the dwelling of Nebmare, Re is a shining disc'. This palace was entirely destroyed, and the American mission which set out to

(*opposite above*) Alabaster lids of the canopic jars which held the mummified viscera of Tutankhamun. Each lid of the four jars is carved in the pharaoh's likeness.
(*opposite below*) A painted box from Tutankhamun's tomb, showing the pharaoh on either side as a crowned sphinx trampling his enemies.

examine it discovered only the foundations and some scattered fragments of pavement.

Amenhotep III had a reason for choosing this particular site and name. Architraves and statues recall the genuine piety which in his youth he felt for his father Amun, but towards the end of his reign there was a visible change of tendency. Amun-Re, lord of Karnak, gradually became less popular than the great sun god of Heliopolis, who showed himself in the form of a disc, *itn*. This was a word which was often to recur under the king's successor. As to the presence of the great priests of Amun of Karnak near by, it was already so awkward that the king avoided them by putting the Nile between himself and such embarrassing dignitaries. The break had not come yet, but the writing was on the wall.

During the Hellenistic era, while the story of Memnon, son of Aurora, was spreading through Egypt, another legend was growing round Amenhotpe, son of Hapu. The great man had acquired a vast reputation for wisdom and learning, and was even accredited with the power of prophecy. This reputation seems not to have been exaggerated. It is quite possible that Amenhotpe was the most learned man of his time. He knew all the geometry and, indeed, all the mathematics that there was to be known in his day. There is no reason to believe that his knowledge did not extend to astronomy.

What were the subjects of conversation between the king and the scholar? The Egyptian texts say nothing, but the Greeks of the Late Period fancied they knew something about it. According to Josephus – or, rather, according to Manetho – Amenhotep III experienced a strong desire to see the gods and turned to Amenhotpe, who seemed to share the divine nature through his wisdom and foresight. Amenhotpe replied that he could realise the king's wish if the king undertook to clear the whole land of lepers and other unclean people. Amenhotpe was a prudent seer, and was afraid of bringing down the anger of the gods on the king and on himself; he also, apparently, foresaw that the Impure and their allies would establish their domination in Egypt for thirteen years.

And that, it is said, was why he chose to kill himself. Actually it is extremely doubtful whether Amenhotpe did in fact kill himself. The whole of this passage in Josephus (Against Apion, 1, 232–6) sounds much more like legend than history. We may just recall that in the Late Period people still remembered the intimacy which once existed between the sage and the king.

If we want a balanced judgment on the great monarch's character, it is better to turn to those who had direct relations with him. Among them was Tushratta, king of Mitanni, who wrote as follows:

To Nimmuaria the great king of Egypt, my brother, my son-in-law who loves you, the king of Mitanni, your brother.

In his day, your father was a friend of my father, but you have increased this friendship even further, and you have been very friendly towards my father; today,

The pharaoh Tutankhamun on a lioness; one of a series of symbolic statuettes found in the tomb. The king wears the white crown of Upper Egypt and carries the kingly flail.

since you and I are on terms of mutual friendship, you have made it ten times closer than with my father.

The king of Mitanni therefore allowed his daughter to return with the Egyptian ambassador, and ended with an urgent request for gold.

When Tushratta learned of the death of Amenhotep III, he wrote to Amenhotep IV: 'When your father was dying I wept and grew ill and almost died, but I learned of the accession of the eldest son of Amenhotep III and of Tiye, and I said: Amenhotep is not dead.'

On this fine testament of friendship let us take leave of Nebmare Amenhotep who reigned for thirty-seven years. He did not let war disturb his empire and he increased the prestige of Egypt at home and abroad.

The Colossi of Memnon, all that remains of the funerary temple of Amenhotep III. The northern one was famous in classical times for its dawn song, until silenced by an earth tremor in the reign of the Emperor Septimus Severus.

4   A heretic and his successor

Amenhotep IV, the enemy of the gods

Amenhotep IV ascended the throne on the death of his father, Amenhotep III, possibly in 1372 BC. It would be helpful if we also knew the king's age, either in 1372, or at the time of his death. Historians have discussed this point without reaching agreement.

The king's initial titulary shows clearly that from his accession he had adopted the tendencies which his father had shown towards the end of his reign. He composed the following names for himself:

> Horus: Valiant bull with tall feathers.
> Vulture-Cobra: Great in royalty at Ipet-Esut.
> Golden Horus: He who raises crowns at Heliopolis in the South.
> The King: Neferkheprure.
> The Son of Re: Amenhotep, sovereign of Thebes.

The third name is the most significant: it proves that Amenhotep IV was crowned on the left bank of the Nile and not in Karnak, his father's favourite domain. Like his father, he wanted to feel that the Nile was between him and the high priests of Amun. In fact, the important thing about his reign, and which makes him unique among the pharaohs, is that he fought against and temporarily destroyed the religion of Amun – and indeed all the old Egyptian religions – and established a new cult. This was the cult of Aten, the disc which sent out rays ending in hands.

At the time of Amenhotep IV's accession, his mother, Queen Tiye, was still alive and was to live with him for some years. He had already married Nefertiti, to whom he remained attached all his life. The sculptors of El-Amarna have given Nefertiti a radiant beauty, the like of which is unknown in Egyptian art. Yet strangely, besides the polychrome statue in Berlin and the statue in Cairo, we have also a sketch on limestone which shows almost nothing of the sovereign's charms. And among all the heads which, rightly or wrongly, are said to be Nefertiti's, none approaches these two masterpieces. It is mainly on the bas-reliefs that she seems to have the same profile as her

A statuette in painted limestone of the heretic pharaoh, Akhenaten, and his queen Nefertiti.

135

Bust of Nefertiti, wife of Akhenaten; the beauty and style in which she is portrayed is very unusual in Egyptian art of the period.

Akhenaten carrying sceptres and wearing a bracelet inscribed with Aten's name.
The emaciated features have been exaggerated to emphasise his inhuman and
therefore godlike quality.

husband, perhaps through mimetism (sculptors were in the habit of giving a wife her husband's features). It may also be that the birth of many children had impaired her beauty.

Who was this Nefertiti? The name may be translated as 'the beautiful woman who has come', and this would be suitable for a foreigner. People have duly maintained that she was Tadukhipa, the daughter of the king of Mitanni, but this has not been proved. The origin of the beautiful queen remains a mystery.

It was only in the year 4 that people began to set up stelae to mark the boundaries of the new royal estate in the fifteenth nome of Upper Egypt. But Amenhotep IV had not waited until the year 4 before opening hostilities against Amun and his priests. At the east of the temple of Amun, where Amenhotep III had undertaken to build a temple in honour of Aten, he had colossal statues raised, which are among the most curious works of Egyptian art. They represent the king wearing the nemer with the uraeus, a square-cut beard, heavy bracelets and pendentives, and holding the sceptre and the flail.

Is he really a pharaoh, this deformed creature, with those unmuscular arms and legs, with a pelvis out of all proportion, a long, narrow face, hollow cheeks and up-turned eyes? There is such an expression of indifference or, rather, disillusionment, that having looked at the best of these statues one cannot ever forget them. The strange thing is that the royal workrooms did not produce such statues any more after the court left Thebes.

An explanation comes to mind. Perhaps Amenhotep IV erected these statues opposite the temple of Amun as the protest of a man who had been cruelly treated by nature, a man whom the gods and their priests had been unable to cure. If these statues had been able to speak, they would have voiced a cold hostility to the gods, who were so hard, so callous about human sufferings. What a mockery to attribute kingship, which demands health and strength and a harmonious stature, to a body which was such an ugly caricature!

As far as we know, the high priests of Amun made no resistance to this royal offensive. They watched passively as their treasure was looted and looked on meekly as the populace defaced the names of Amun on all the bas-reliefs, while the more agile among them climbed up to do the same on the tops of the obelisks. Traditionally, the high priests had means of defending themselves, for we know of leaders, lieutenants, scribes, and soldiers of the temple of Amun; but Egypt had not disdained the profession of arms for forty years with impunity. Besides, most Egyptians had no inclination for it. While the Hyksos had been oppressing Egypt as far as Cusae, there had, indeed, been men to lead the bravest soldiers of Upper Egypt against the invader. Men like Kamose, Ahmose, and Amenhotep I had driven out the Hyksos; and, after them, Thutmose III and the sportsmen-kings, Amenhotep II and Thutmose IV, had kept the spirit of conquest alive in Egypt. But Amenhotep III had allowed this inheritance to be endangered, and now Amenhotep IV was reduced to enrolling foreign mercenaries for his bodyguard. One can guess that these Nubians, Libyans and Syrians were not gentle with the native population.

In the year 6 the court abandoned the old capital and installed itself at the place now known as El-Amarna. This was exactly half-way between Heliopolis in the North and Heliopolis in the South, the points of departure and arrival for the colossi of Memnon. When Amenhotep had summoned his friends, the great officers of his palace, and his soldiers, he solemnly announced that this was the site of the new capital. In fact it did not belong to any god or goddess, king or queen. The great officers approved, as always; and the king raised his hands towards heaven, towards his father the god, and called on him to witness his oath.

I shall make Akhetaten [the glory of Aten] for Aten my father, neither further south, nor further north, nor further east, nor further west. I shall not go beyond the frontiers in the south or in the north, nor shall I build in the west, but I shall build in the east where the sun appears, in the place he has chosen to ring with mountains . . . If the queen were to tell me that there was a finer place for Aten, I should not listen to her.

And he ended by saying that wherever he or the queen might die, they must be interred at Akhetaten.[1]

Another frontier stele proclaims the new names of the king and queen:

> Long live the Horus, valiant bull beloved of Aten.
> The Vulture-Cobra, great in sovereignty in Akhetaten.
> The Golden Horus, exalting the name of Aten.
> The King: Neferkheprure [lovely are the forms of Re].
> Waenre [the One and Only of Re].
> The Son of Re: Akhenaten [glorious for Aten].
> The hereditary princess . . . The great royal wife, his beloved: Nefernefruaten [Beautiful is the beauty of Aten] Nefertiti.

Then comes the great oath:

As truly as my father Aten is living, I will make Akhetaten for my father Aten in this place. I will not make Akhetaten for him in the south, or in the north, or in the west, or in the east . . . The space which lies between these four stelae is truly Akhetaten. It belongs to Aten the father: mountains, deserts, prairies, islands, upper soil and lower soil, land, water, villages, men and animals, and everything which my father Aten brings into life eternally and for ever. I shall never break this vow which I have made to Aten my father, for ever.[2]

Akhenaten moved in with his family and courtiers and began to build the new city immediately. He commissioned the best work-leaders in the country, and the technicians who, in a matter of months, were to make a city, with all its essential features, rise from the earth: the temple, the king's palace, the queen's palace, the officials' houses, the workrooms, and the residences of the important functionaries.

The temple was situated in a vast enclosure measuring eight hundred by three hundred yards. There are only traces of this enclosure left but these are enough to show that there were no hypostyle rooms or closed rooms, but that everything, including the great altar and the tables of offerings, was open to the air. One can imagine the king, followed by the queen and the princesses, as he advances towards the altar. He would raise his hands towards the daystar and recite this famous hymn:

Thou arisest beauteous in the horizon of heaven, O living Aten, beginner of life when thou dost shine forth in the eastern horizon and dost fill every land with thy beauty.

Thou art comely, great, sparkling, and high above every land, and thy rays enfold the lands to the limit of all that thou hast made, thou being the sun, and thou reachest their limits and subjectest them to thy beloved son.

Being afar off, yet thy rays are upon the earth. Thou art in men's faces, yet thy movements are unseen. When thou settest in the western horizon, the earth is in darkness after the manner of death. The night is passed in the bedchamber, heads covered, no eye can see its fellow. Their belongings are stolen, even though they be under their heads, and they perceive it not. Every lion is come forth from its lair and all snakes bite. Darkness is [the sole] illumination while the earth is silence, their maker resting in his horizon.

The earth grows bright, when thou hast arisen in the horizon, shining as Aten in the daytime. Thou banishest darkness and bestowest thy rays. The Two Lands are in festival, awakened they stand on their feet, thou hast lifted them up. Their limbs are cleansed, clothes put on, and their hands are upraised in praise at thy glorious appearing. The entire land does its work. All cattle are at peace upon their pastures. Trees and pastures grow green. Birds, taking flight on their wings, give praise to thy spirit. All animals frisk upon their feet. All that flyeth or alighteth live when thou arisest for them. Ships fare north and likewise fare south. Every road is opened at thy appearing. The fish in the river leap before thy face. Thy rays are in the Great-Green. Who causest the female fluid to grow in women and who makest the water in mankind; bringing to life the son in the body of his mother; soothing him by the cessation of his tears; nurse [already] in the body, who givest air to cause to live all whom thou makest, and the child descendeth from the body to breathe on the day of his birth; thou openest his mouth fully and makest this sustenance. The chick in the egg speaketh in the shell; thou givest him air in it to make him live; thou hast made for him his completion so as to break it, even the egg, and he cometh forth from the egg to speak of his completion, and he walketh upon his two feet when he comes forth from it.

How manifold are thy works. They are mysterious in men's sight. Thou sole god, like to whom there is none other. Thou didst create the earth after thy heart, being alone, even all men, herds and flocks, whatever is upon earth, creatures that walk upon feet, which soar aloft flying with their wings, the countries of Khor and of Cush, and the land of Egypt. Thou settest every man in his place, and makest their sustenance, each one possessing his food, and his term of life counted; tongues made diverse in speech and their characters likewise; their complexions distinguished, for thou hast distinguished country and country.

Thou makest the Nile-flood in the netherworld, and bringest it at thy pleasure to give life to the common folk, even as thou makest them for thyself, the lord of them all who travailest with them; the lord of every land who shinest for them, the Aten of the daytime, great of majesty. All distant lands, thou hast made their life. Thou has set a Nile-flood in the sky, and it descendeth for them and maketh waves upon the mountains like the Great-Green to drench their fields in their villages. How efficacious are thy plans, thou lord of eternity. A Nile-flood in heaven, it is thy gift to the foreign countries and to the animals of every country which walk upon feet. But the Nile-flood comes forth from the netherworld for the land of Egypt. Thy rays foster every mead. When thou shinest forth, they live and they grow for thee.

Thou makest the seasons in order to prosper all that thou hast made, the winter to cool them, the summer-heat that they may taste of thee. Thou hast made the sky distant to shine in it and to see all that thou hast made, being alone and shining in thy various forms as the living Aten, appearing gloriously and gleaming, being both distant and near. Thou makest millions of forms out of thee alone, towns and villages, fields, roads, and river. Every eye beholds thee in front of it, thou being the disk of the daytime. . . .

There is none other that knoweth thee except thy son Neferkheprure-waenre. Thou hast caused him to be skilled in thy ways and in thy strength. The earth comes into being upon thy hand even as thou makest them. Thou hast shone forth and they live. Thou settest and they die. Thou thyself art life and men live by thee. Eyes are in presence of beauty until thou settest. All work is laid aside when thou settest since thou didst found the earth. Thou raisest them up for thy son who came forth from thy body, the King of Upper and Lower Egypt, living on Truth, the lord of the Two Lands Neferkheprure-waenre, the son of Re, living on Truth, lord of glorious appearings, Akhenaten great in his duration; with the king's great wife, whom he loves, the lady of the Two lands, Nefernefruaten-Nefertiti, may she live and flourish for ever and ever.

One cannot fail to recognise the beauty of this hymn, for all its repetitions and clumsy expressions. What emerges from it is that Akhenaten had completely rejected the ancient gods of Egypt, including Osiris and Isis (the most engaging pair in the pantheon), along with the popular Hathor, Ptah the demiurge, and Thoth, the master of heavenly words. The old names of the solar god, the crowns, the pilgrimages and the solar barges, they are all cast aside like useless trappings. Henceforward there is only one god, Aten, the disc with bountiful rays, and we must admit that Akhenaten found delightful images to evoke its benefits, like the images of the birds and baboons running joyfully in front of the rising sun. It is remarkable to learn that the Syrians and Nubians benefit from Aten's goodness as well of the Egyptians; but, after all, the great, the only real beneficiaries of this goodness are the king and his beloved queen, for they are in the centre of creation.

The buildings of Akhetaten are made mostly of unburnt brick, and since the builders were in a hurry, it was the best thing to use. All the walls and pillars were coated with creamy stucco or with white lime decorated with scenes from private life. The paving was decorated like the walls. In a room attached to the harem there was a picture of a great rectangular pool with birds and fish among the nenuphars. Between the columns there were more bushes and birds, and higher up there were other shrubs and thickets round which calves were gambolling with the best grace in the world. When this decoration was intact, it must have been a delight to look upon. The bushes have been drawn with a freedom and fantasy which Egyptian artists had not shown before, even in their best works. Must we attribute this to the influence of Minoan art? It has not been proved, and I shall simply note that these lovely pictures are the pictorial translation of certain passages in the hymn. It was in the private palace that Flinders Petrie discovered and very skilfully removed the fragments which are now at the Ashmolean Museum in Oxford, the undoubted gems of Egyptian painting. There is nothing more delicate, nothing more disarming than those two little girls on cushions beside their parents, exchanging their grave and innocent caresses.

Tomb-painting showing two daughters of Akhenaten and Nefertiti; life at court was depicted with full naturalism in accordance with the aim of 'living in truth'.

Aten the bountiful did not grant the royal couple the male heir they no doubt wanted. In compensation he gave them six little girls, one of whom, however, Meketaten, died in infancy. The king, holding the queen by the arm, went to the child's deathbed, and they both struck their heads in sign of mourning.

The royal family were devoted to each other, and the artists did not refrain from representing intimate scenes in their family life. In one representation, Akhenaten, Nefertiti and some of the princesses have gone to visit the Queen Mother Tiye. They have found her in good health and are drinking from goblets together. The princesses are not drinking but they have discovered a pile of fruit, and they are helping themselves, with or without permission. If the king wants to drink, he holds out his goblet and the queen herself pours the fiery liquid through a strainer. We are also shown the royal couple taking refreshment: the king is avidly eating a leg or shoulder of lamb, and the queen is eating goose or duck.

Whether they are going to the temple, or just going for a walk, the ceremonial hardly ever changes. First comes the royal guard, which includes soldiers from all parts, each of them bearing an ensign; then comes the king's

Relief from Tel el-Amarna showing
Akhenaten and Nefertiti.

chariot, then the queen's, and those of the princesses and courtiers. On one occasion the king and queen are together in the same chariot, and if I am not mistaken Nefertiti is about to kiss her husband.

With Akhenaten spending most of his time in devotions and family pleasures, what remained for public affairs? Perhaps he thought that these would be better taken care of if he left them alone. Besides, there were offices of scribes busy revictualling the capital, bringing in the taxes and receiving and answering mail. From time to time Akhenaten would thank these worthy functionaries according to the familiar ceremonial. He would show himself with the queen and princesses on the balcony of state, and toss goblets and necklets to the fortunate recipient. The man would put the necklets over his head and leave the palace to be acclaimed by his friends.

In the year 12 there was a grandiose ceremony, such as there had often been in the time of Thutmose III and the warrior kings. Delegates from neighbouring lands came to beg for the breath of life and to present offerings to the king. Akhenaten arrived in a litter. He dismounted and took his place under a canopy which had been set up in a place large enough to hold all the visitors.

In the year 12, the second month of the winter, the 8th, King Akhenaten and the great royal wife Nefertiti living for ever show themselves on a golden chair to receive the merchandise of Syria, Nubia, the West and the East. All the lands are brought together, the isles in the midst of the sea present their products to the king on the great throne of Akhenaten. The works of all the lands are received, and Akhenaten grants the breath of life.[3]

One does indeed see Nubians, Libyans, Asiatics and other foreigners among the crowd, and some gifts as well, though the gifts are not as numerous as they were in the reign of Thutmose III. And so the happy days of Akhetaten continued, and Aten still watched over his own.

Akhenaten died after a reign of eighteen years. He had a tomb prepared for himself in a wady to the east of his city, but the tomb was pillaged and degraded, and no one knows what happened to his mummy and his funerary furniture, except for a few statuettes and some fragments of a sarcophagus.

Certainly Akhenaten was not a great king like Thutmose III and those who pushed back the frontiers of Egypt. Yet, in the long series of pharaohs, he is unique. Before him, Egypt had been governed by moralist kings, of vaguely monotheistic tendencies, for they spoke more often of the god than they did of the gods. But no one else had dared to proclaim that since the sun is the author of nature, since the sun alone gives life to creation, it is to the sun alone that our prayers and offerings should be made. Akhenaten was not just a philosopher, he was a poet and an artist; he was not just a connoisseur of painting and sculpture, he was a musician who liked to hear his choir of blind singers and the sound of his new harps. Artists gave his ephemeral capital a brilliance beyond comparison. What the king had done by shaking off the

Mourners at a funerary shrine, shown in another wall-painting in the royal sculptors' tomb at Thebes.

Painting of a funeral ceremony from the tomb of Metamun and Ipuki, sculptors to Akhenaten and Tutankhamun.

farrago of old rites, sculptors like Thutmose, Beki and their followers had done for the rigid rules which encumbered art. They had brought it something irreplaceable: freedom.

If Amenhotep had not existed, our gallery of famous pharaohs would lack its most original figure.

Tutankhamun, the restorer of the cult of Amun

Akhenaten, who died after a reign of eighteen years, wanted to be succeeded by his son-in-law, Smenkhkare, who had married his eldest daughter. Smenkhkare's reign was brief, and it brought no real changes. When he died (perhaps before his father-in-law), it was the turn of Tutankhamun, 'pleasant is the life of Amun', husband of the third daughter of Akhenaten and Nefertiti: Ankhesnpaten, 'her life belongs to Aten'. The new king seems also to have had a more direct claim to the royal inheritance. He may have been the son of Amenhotep III, and therefore the dead king's brother. On a red granite lion which originally guarded the temple of Soleb, a lion which was dragged to Napata and may now be seen in the British Museum, one does in fact read: 'King Tutankhamun who restored the monuments of his father Nebmare, Tet-Re Amenhotep, sovereign of Thebes'. Other scholars believe

(*above*) Lion from Gebel Barkal in the Sudan, originally dedicated by Tutankhamun in the Temple of Soleb.

(*opposite*) Head of the fallen colossus of Ramses II, described by Herodotus, which stood near the temple of Ptah at Mit Rahina, the ancient city of Memphis.

he was the son of Akhenaten by an unofficial marriage. I believe, however, that there is no reason to doubt a statement of such clarity as that on the lion. The princely child must therefore have been born very late in the reign of Amenhotep the Magnificent – perhaps he was even born a few months after his death. He was undoubtedly much attached to the memory of his parents, as we know from two precious relics discovered in his tomb: a solid gold statuette of Amenhotep III and a lock of hair cut from Queen Tiye when she was a child. However, on the death of Amenhotep III, Tiye may have been too old to have children. Some authors consider that Tutankhamun's mother was Princess Sitamun, who presented the two handsome chairs found in the tomb of Yuia and Tjuia. One wonders if Tiye had asked the princess to take her place and give a last child to Amenhotep III. As the child of an elderly father, Tutankhamun was frail, and his expectation of life was short. If he was actually born in the same year that Amenhotep IV came to the throne, he would have been seventeen or eighteen when he himself became king. This may be the case, but one must remember that when Tutankhamun's mummy was solemnly examined by Dr Derry in the presence of the Egyptian authorities, the examination revealed that Tutankhamun was not more than twenty when he died, and must therefore have been eleven in the year of his coronation (which supports the theory that he was Akhenaten's son). This is very young to have taken the great decisions which had to be taken. Whatever the truth may be, he reigned, and he died extremely young.

The statues of Tutankhamun which were found in his tomb, like the lay figure, and the head which emerges from a lotus-flower, are the likenesses of a very young boy.[1] Of course the king might well have kept statues from the 'Amarnian period' of his reign to be laid, eventually, in his tomb. But the famous statue which was found in the favissa at Karnak would be right for a young man of twenty or so.[2] The head and torso are in perfect condition. A statue of the god Chons, which was also found at Karnak, is an almost exact reproduction of it. The resemblance of the two statues to the original is therefore guaranteed. The features are regular, the eyes are turned up towards the temples, the lips are thick but not excessively so. The body is rather frail, which is not surprising, but if Tutankhamun was not an athlete, at least he did not show any of the defects which had afflicted Akhenaten.

We have no statues of the queen. She is painted with the king on the backs of some chairs and on certain articles in the tomb. She was very pretty. Possibly one of the female heads found at El-Amarna is of her, but we cannot prove it. The king and queen led a peaceful existence until the end of the reign, and no other woman, apparently, played the slightest part in the king's life.

The king was crowned at Akhctatcn, and he died at Thebes in the year 9 of his reign. In the interval he became reconciled with Amun. This reconciliation was necessary, as Amenhotep IV had only converted a few of his subjects to

Queen Nofretari playing chess in the Underworld; a painted relief from the entrance to her tomb in the Valley of the Tombs of the Queens.

his ideas. The rest of Egypt, deprived of Amun, was like a ship without a pilot. But who was the first to put forward the idea, the king or his advisers? The reconciliation could not have taken place without a great deal of bargaining. No doubt there were wise men in Thebes and Akhetaten who explained convincingly that a house divided against itself must fall. That could be said of Egypt. She was threatened from the north and south by neighbours who were quite capable of joining forces against her, as had been done in the times of the Hyksos. The final decision was officially the king's, who alone had the army at his disposal. However, one day in the year 3 or 4, the king, who was from now on to be called Tutankhamun, 'pleasant is the life of Amun' (his wife was now called Ankhesnamun, 'her life is Amun's'), embarked on the royal ship. The troops also embarked and, together, they set out for Thebes, the queen of cities. There is no proof that the population went before Tutankhamun waving sistrums and flowers, as they had done for Seti I when he returned from his victories in the land of Canaan. But there is no proof, either, that Tutankhamun had to appear as a culprit before the high priests of Amun, and that he received a cool reception. Those who have suggested this have forgotten that there were no longer any priests of Amun. The last Ptahmose had died in the days of Amenhotep III, and he does not seem to have been replaced. Amun's property had been confiscated, and the faithful had been dispersed. The other gods had not been treated any better. For a quarter of a century the pharaoh had forgotten to make nominations, and nothing was any longer kept up. On the great stela on which he sums up his deeds, Tutankhamun himself undertook to paint the state of the country:

When His Majesty was crowned king, the temples of the gods and goddesses had been abandoned, from Elephantine to the marshes of the Delta; their holy dwellings had been laid waste and had fallen into ruin . . . Their sanctuaries no longer existed, and their houses were thoroughfares. The land was in decline, because the gods neglected the land. Their hearts were pining so in their bodies, that they let creation pine away . . .[3]

When the Egyptians wanted to express the desolate state of the country, they could only use the clichés which had been in circulation for so long, since the time of the god. These clichés still applied. The most urgent matter was to restore the cult of Amun, Ptah and the other gods. Tutankhamun consecrated statues to them, he gave them possessions, and he built them monuments which surpassed all the ones that had gone before.

Several of the great monuments executed on his orders have been found at Karnak, first and foremost the statue of the god Chons, to whom the king gave his own likeness, then a statue of Amun protecting Tutankhamun, which is now in the Louvre.[4] The king's head has been broken, probably out of hostility, but the god's head, which is another portrait of the king, remains intact. As long as the sculptors were confined to Akhenaten, they had had nothing to do but portray the king and queen and princesses, and many examples of their skill have been found in the house of Thutmose and Beki. But now they were free, as they had been in the good old days, to associate the king and the gods in the most varied ways. It was perhaps in the sculptors' studios that there was most rejoicing at this return to the old ways.

We do not know the names of the great priests of Amun, Ptah and the other gods who were now appointed, who had the onerous task of beginning things again after an interval of more than twenty years. But thanks to the inscriptions and paintings on the tomb of Huy (number 40 at Thebes), we can see Tutankhamun appointing some very important functionaries.[5]

The king is wearing his great robes of state, and is seated under a canopy. Huy, laden with bouquets, is about to leave the audience chamber, surrounded and acclaimed by his friends. Before he leaves, the chief of the double treasure informs him of the vast extent of the domain over which he will exercise his authority, from the nome of Nekhen, the second in Upper Egypt, to the Seats of the Two Lands, otherwise known as Gebel Barkal. Other functionaries hand him his seal of office and parchments. Such a post could only have been given to a man who had earned the confidence of the king and that of Amun, and perhaps Huy was one of those who had shown a gift for negotiations early on in the reign. He had also earned this confidence by bringing the Retjnu delegates, with their presents, from Syria (it would soon be the turn of the queen and princes of the South, bringing animals and exotic commodities and a great quantity of gold, carnelian and ivory). Huy had also brought some prisoners, their arms bound behind their backs; he had certainly earned his congratulations from the palace and the grand temple of Amun.

Tutankhamun was rightly proud to compare the old order with the state of things in his own time:

If messages were sent to the Djahi to enlarge the frontiers of Egypt, they had no success. . . . But since His Majesty has received the seal of his father, and governed the territory of Horus, the black land [the valley of the Nile] and the red land [the desert] have been under his dominion.

One of the fortunate effects of Tutankhamun's policy was the resumption of trade with Byblos. In the time of Akhenaten, the king of Byblos, Rib-Addi, had been careful not to break off relations with Egypt; but, beset by many cruel enemies, Rib-Addi had not been able to send his men into the mountains to fell trees and drag them all the way to Byblos. Now, once again, the timber was to pile up on the quay at Karnak. The land of Negau, which is mentioned as early as dynasty VI, included the forest land from Byblos to the valley of the Eleuthere. Pinewood and spruce were found there, cedar and juniper. From time to time the king of Byblos had sent his woodcutters there and these trees too were dragged to Byblos and sent to Egypt.

One must be very careful to distinguish the votive barges which were housed in the temple storerooms and carried in processions, from the 'barges on the river', which were made for navigation and were veritable floating temples. The 'barges on the river' were given names like buildings. And so the barge of Amun was called Amun-Usir-Hat, 'Amun of the strong heart', and the barge of Ptah at Memphis was called Neb heh-n: 'master of eternity'. The latter was a hundred cubits long. Since the beginning of dynasty XVIII, each pharaoh had wanted to gain renown by building new and more spacious barges. Tutankhamun had to make up for some delay, and he showed great energy in this respect.

The preparations for the great feast of Opet, alone, called for the building of the barges of Amun, Mut and Chons, as well as the barges of the king and queen and their household. The barge of Amun, the biggest, was embellished fore and aft with two rams' heads (the ram was dedicated to Amun); the barge of Mut with two women's heads surmounted by a vulture. The barge of Chons had two falcons' heads. But their decoration did not consist merely of these figures. The hull was covered with bas-reliefs down to the waterline: these bas-reliefs gave representations of the king accomplishing the prescribed rites for Amun and the paredres gods. In front of the great house on the bridge – as if it were a real temple – were a pair of obelisks, and masts with pennants. Wherever room could be found, there stood a sphinx or a statue. Everything was streaming with gold and jewels.

In the intervals between the great feasts, these ponderous vessels were sensibly anchored in their docks near the temples of Amun, Mut and Chons. When the time arrived, a veritable army of soldiers and sailors would drag them out, not without difficulty, but taking advantage of the high water in the middle of the season of the floods, while a vast crowd assembled on the quay. A hymn to Amun was recited. Women waved sistrums and crotalums, men beat tambourines. Nubians whirled round in dances. Trumpets were borne among the crowds by soldiers with feathers stuck in their hair. Then the critical moment was over. The royal barge, the divine barges and their suite were afloat on the waters of the Nile. They were attached to towing barges which were equipped with sails. The chief cracked his whip. Sightseers had come from all over the country to enjoy the spectacle. Tents and refreshment booths had been set up along the banks, wherever there was room. Food and drink were constantly arriving. Fruit was brought, and terebinth (*sonter*) to cleanse the air while animals were slaughtered and cut up; the cooks can rarely have been out of work. The soldiers, warmed by the food and drink, beat their tambourines even harder while dancing women with bare breasts turned cartwheels to the compulsive rhythm.

Slowly the fleet made its way towards the southern Opet, Luxor, where it stayed for several days. We have no idea of how the time was spent. Perhaps there were performances of some of Amun's struggles with other gods, like

Set. And then it was time to think of the journey back; the stalls were still open, but enthusiasm was beginning to wane. The portable barges were put back in their cases. The passengers, led by the king, walked through the avenue of rams to return thanks to the king of gods and to all the triad. The king was assured of a long future, the length of days of Re, the function of Tum, years of eternity on the throne of Horus in joy and valour, victory over every land, and the strength of his father Amun.[6]

But in fact the king's days were numbered. Unlike certain other Egyptologists, I think Tutankhamun made good use of the few years which he was allowed to spend on the throne of Horus. He ended a schism which was destroying Egypt. The moment he returned to Karnak, he began to make the necessary appointments. He erected statues, and he put up the fine stela which gives a summary of his actions. The resumption of trade with Syria was an extremely important event. Tutankhamun was also able to reorganise the Theban fleet. For the first time in twenty years the sacred barges were launched on the Nile, to the acclamations of the delighted crowd. The king did not want to let such a remarkable ceremony fall into oblivion and decided to have the chief episodes sculpted on the outer side of the long wall of the temple of Luxor. The king and queen and the highest authorities took part in this festival, and it sealed the reconciliation of the monarchy, the people, and the most powerful of the Egyptian gods. For some ten years all the king's decisions had been made with this result in mind.

In returning to Thebes, restoring the cult of Amun and the ancient gods was not Tutankhamun's only motive. He was also thinking of his eternal dwelling. He considered building it in the Valley of Kings, near the dwellings of his illustrious ancestors.

The tomb of a king, at any period, always consists of two elements: the temple destined for his cult and for that of the gods of the necropolis, and the tomb itself. In the days of the Old Kingdom, the temple and the tomb were one and the same. The kings of dynasty xviii had adopted the habit of building their funerary temple on the left bank of Thebes, facing the rising sun. At the time we are speaking of now, the temples of Amenhotep i, Queen Hatshepsut, Thutmose iii and Thutmose iv were no doubt used again for their old purpose, like the temples on the right bank. The most magnificent was the temple of Amenhotep iii – which the colossi of Memnon still brings to mind. Amenhotpe, son of Hapu, had been allowed to build his own temple close beside it, and Tutankhamun had already chosen a site in the immediate vicinity.

In troubled times, it occasionally happened that buildings did not remain dedicated to their builder for long. Was the temple of Tutankhamun finished when he died? We do not know, but it was certainly taken over by Ay, Tutankhamun's successor, who also soon had to give place to Haremhab, the ambitious character with whom we end dynasty xviii.

The Oriental Institute of Chicago, which undertook research in the section between the temple of Amenhotep III and Medinet Habu, found the ruins of a building which was at first thought to be the temple of Ay, usurped by Haremhab. This building was really Tutankhamun's funerary temple. The American mission found the remains of two quartzite statues of Tutankhamun which had been taken over by Haremhab. A magnificent head of Tutankhamun, from a private collection, was presented to the Academy of Inscriptions by M. Cl. Schaeffer, which almost certainly belongs to one of these two statues. We can therefore say that Tutankhamun's funerary temple was usurped by Ay and usurped again by Haremhab.

At the end of dynasty XVIII, the Valley of Kings was not yet cluttered up with fifty-eight hypogeums, leaving little room for anything else. There were only ten tombs, quite a distance from each other. Tutankhamun's only problem was which site to choose, and he simply picked a place near the spot where the road which comes up from the cultivated lands enters the royal cemetery.

A very steep flight of stairs leads down into the tomb. It is one of the smallest tombs in the Valley of Kings, and one is struck by the disproportion between the restricted space and the opulence of the funerary furniture. Presumably the chief quarryman at the necropolis had meant to add further chambers to those which exist, but the king's death had put an end to the plan. While the embalmers were preparing the royal mummy – they had twelve days to do so – the stone sarcophagi were put in position, one inside the other, with the gilt wood chapels which protected them. The day of the funeral arrived. The mummy was taken down into the vault in the presence of King Ay, Tutankhamun's successor, who 'opened the mouth'. When the coffin was in place, all the doors were shut and the entrance to the tomb was walled up. Before this was done, a coffer with an Anubis and numerous other things on top had been laid in a small adjoining chamber. The seals of the necropolis were set on the wall, and two wooden sentinels, painted in asphalt, representing Tutankhamun, were left to keep guard over the dead king.

It was now a question of arranging the funerary furniture as well as possible in the two narrow chambers. The set of furniture seems quite splendid and abundant, but this is because we are comparing it with what archaeologists have found in desecrated or poorer tombs; but Thutmose III or Amenhotep III would not have had any cause to envy their descendant. Once the adjoining chambers were full, three large state beds were set against the far wall of the great chamber; they had obviously been made in the same workroom, and they assured the dead man of the protection of the cow Hathor, lady of the West, of the Lion which, though fearsome in itself, is also an agent of resurrection, and of the Hippopotamus Thueris, which not only protects little children but wards off evil influences during sleep.

Tutankhamun's gold coffin from his tomb in the Valley of Kings.
(*overleaf*) The heads of Tutankhamun and his wife from the back of the gilt throne.

(*opposite*) Scenes of court life as depicted on a gold shrine from the tomb of Tutankhamun.

Back of a cedarwood chair from Tutankhamun's tomb; the openwork decoration depicts a spirit, symbolising millions of years, kneeling on the sign of the gold necklet.

(*above*) Ostrich feather fan from the tomb, as found by Carter.

(*below*) The sacred goose of Amun made of wood covered with black varnish.

(*right*) Alabaster statuette of the
protective god Bes, found in the tomb.
His crown forms a vase.

(*below*) A vase shaped like a pomegranate
from the pharaoh's tomb.

Tutankhamun's sandals, decorated with figures of his enemies, so that he literally trod on his foes as he walked.

The essentials had been performed. Maspero wrote, very justly, that the Egyptians conceived a burial as if it was moving house. The carriers entrusted with this extraordinary removal were, perhaps, pressed for time and space, and they deposited the most diverse objects – coffers, dismantled chariots and seats – under and on top of the great state beds. The first visitors to the tomb were astonished to see a lattice-work bed of the simplest kind which had been thrown on top of the great bed of Hathor and pierced by one of the cow's magnificent horns. And yet nothing – or hardly anything – was spoilt. When their task was done, the carriers withdrew, and thenceforward a wall prevented anyone from entering the wonderful tomb.

When Ramses VI dug his hypogeum a few yards away, the excavations soon revealed the entrance to Tutankhamun's tomb. In the interval this entrance had become accessible, and it was guarded only by the keepers of the necropolis. There were therefore some attempts to break in. They failed, and no doubt the malefactors were severely punished, for no more attempts were made.

I imagine that the king's mourning rites followed the usual form. Everyday affairs were carried on by a divine father called Ay, who had been an important official in the days of Akhenaten. He had already prepared his own tomb in the southern necropolis of Akhetaten, but he abandoned this tomb and also his legitimate wife, who had been the queen's nurse, when a more brilliant future presented itself. He was not afraid to make advances to Tutankhamun's widow, who was presumably still young and charming. She wrote to the most powerful king of the time, the Hittite king Suppiluliumas, saying that since she had been widowed without giving birth to a son, she was exposed to marrying one of her slaves. The Hittite king did not answer at once, but after a second message he sent a young prince to Egypt – a prince who was killed before he achieved his aim. Queen Ankhesnamun resigned herself to her fate and married Ay, as is proved by a ring on the bezel of which the names of Ay and Ankhesnamun are joined.

And so ends the prodigious adventure which had begun, some twenty-five years earlier, when Amenhotep IV decided to forswear the faith of his fathers.

5 Greatness and decline

Ramses II, the Great

Ramses II reigned for sixty-seven years. His reign, with that of Pepi II, is probably the longest in the history of the pharaohs. Its length is attested by Manetho, and confirmed by ostraca and, in particular, by a stela on which Ramses IV wishes himself a reign as long as the sixty-seven years of Ramses II. Something is always missing from these chronological statements. We do not know either the date of his accession to the throne, or the date of his death. There is a further cause of uncertainty, for Ramses II was the second son of Seti I, and he became hereditary prince only on the death of his elder brother. His reign occurred approximately in the first three-quarters of the thirteenth century BC.

Ramses II is the third king of dynasty XIX. This new dynasty took possession of the throne after the death of Haremhab. Haremhab had married Ankhesnamun, the widow of Tutankhamun and Ay, but he had died without an heir. The founder of the dynasty, Ramses I, belonged to a family of the eastern Delta where for generations all the men had been called Seti or Ramses; they served a god who was not sympathetic to all Egyptians. This god was the enemy of Amun and the murderer of Osiris: the god Set, lord of Avaris, the old capital of the Hyksos. Despite these antecedents, which were enough to keep him from the throne for some time, the future Ramses I managed to gain the confidence of Haremhab and that of the people of Thebes. On his accession he took the names of Menpehtire Ramesse; it is possible that he gave his name (his coronation name) to what the Greek astronomers called the Menophres era, which begins in about 1321 BC. Here at last is a definite date.[1] Ramses I was already old, and he had a short reign of only one or two years, but his reign was well filled; he undertook the building of the hypostyle room at Karnak, a temple at Gurnah and another at Abydos, and he chose a place in the Valley of Kings for his tomb. In order to show his gratitude to the god of Mesen, he raised a monument to him on the eastern frontier. The pedestal of this monument has been reconstructed in the Garden of Stelae at Ismailia.[2] Ramses I also showed his foresight by associating

Bas-relief from Abydos showing Seti making offerings to the sun god Horus.

his son Seti in his government, if not at the very beginning, at least from the second and last year of his reign.

Seti I introduced the epithet *whm mswt*, 'the renewer of births', as his Nebty-name in his titulary (the name had already been used by Amenemnes I, the founder of dynasty XII). He wanted to emphasise that an exhausted family, without a male heir, was being replaced by a family assured of a long future. His wife, Queen Tuia, gave him at least five children, of whom the second, Ramses, was his successor.

The reign of Seti I was glorious; he fought victoriously in Syria and Nubia. In order to reassure the Egyptians, who might have been deterred by his worship of Set – and equally, out of personal piety – he built a sumptuous temple in the city of Osiris, at Abydos, where his father had already raised a sanctuary. This temple is one of the finest monuments in Egypt. It proved not only Seti's devotion to the most popular Egyptian god, but his determination to associate himself with the seventy-six kings who had created Egypt; it also proved his desire to associate his son, the royal prince Ramses, who is shown standing beside him, reciting formulae from a roll of papyrus. On another bas-relief at the temple of Abydos, the young prince and his father are taking part in an important rite: lassooing the ox 'neg', the male of the South, for the king.[3] While Seti is throwing his lassoo on a running neg, the royal son has skilfully seized its tail, as if to conform to an old text on the pyramids: 'Hail to thee, neg of negs, when you appear, N takes you by the tail. He seizes you by the horns.' And so when Seti I had the temple of Abydos decorated, he knew that his successor would be Prince Ramses, and he took the greatest care with

Relief from Abydos showing Ramses II and one of his sons taking part in the rite of capturing a bull.

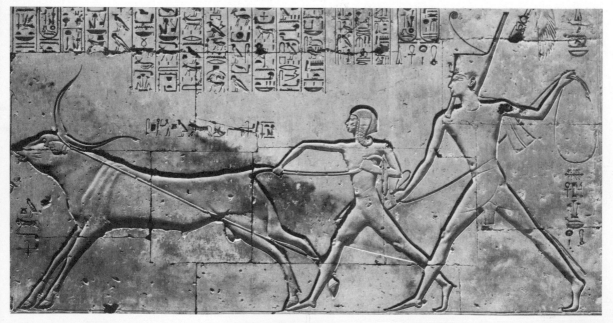

his education. As in the days of Thutmose III and Amenhotep II, this education was, above all, that of a sportsman and warrior, but it also included certain theories of history and politics, and also of religious practices, to enable him to fulfil his various duties.

In the great dedicatory inscription at Abydos, an obscure passage suggests that the king had surrounded the young prince with ladies-in-waiting who in their beauty rivalled the girls in the palace. Perhaps, even now, he had chosen a wife for him from among the women in the harem.

When the king felt that his days were numbered, he decided to present his son to the people. He held him in his arms, saying: 'Crown him king, so that I may see his power while I am alive.' Then the courtiers were summoned to set the diadems on his brow. ' "Put the crown on his head," he said, speaking of me, when he was on earth, "so that he may rule and administer this country . . ." So spake he, weeping, because of the great love he bore me in his heart.'[4] While the young sovereign was receiving the crowns and the insignia of his function, the names which were introduced in the titulary were enumerated to the household couriers so that, in their turn, they could inform the chiefs of the nomes and missions:

> Horus name: Mighty bull, beloved of Maat.
> Vulture-Cobra: Protector of Egypt, chastiser of foreign lands.
> Golden Horus: Rich in years, great in victories.
> King: Usimare-setpenre; Strong is the truth of Re, Elect of Re. (The king is very often designated by his fourth name.)
> Son of Re: Ramesse-miamun; Re has put thee into the world. Beloved of Amun.

Seti I had prepared a magnificent tomb for himself, one of the biggest and the best decorated in the whole Valley of Kings. There is a remarkable picture in a room near the entrance. It shows the four human races in the presence of Horus: the Asiatics with pointed beards and waist-cloths of many colours; the Negroes, the Libyans, and finally the Men – that is to say the Egyptians.

The abundance and richness of the furniture was matched by the beauty of the decoration, but no doubt the tomb was one of the first to be pillaged by the bandits who laid waste to the whole necropolis during the last years of dynasty XX. Later, the coffin was removed and the king's mummy, stripped of its ornaments, was laid in another coffin, of cedarwood. Statements in hieratic script were put in the coffin each time the mummy was moved. The earliest of these statements dates from Herihor, who was still only a high priest of Amun: it is simply about renewing the shrouding. In the second statement, Herihor is king. In the year 16 Seti was transferred from his tomb to the tumulus of Queen Inhapy. The third statement, according to date, is that of the last Pinudjem, when he was brought into the burial-place. The body, wrapped in strong yellowish cloth, was in a remarkable state of preservation. The head was coated in tar, and was almost that of a living man. It stayed there until the memorable day in the history of archaeology, when the royal burial-place was found and emptied of its contents by the Service des Antiquités.[5]

While the embalmers were practising their arts on the king's mummy, the court observed strict mourning. Then at last came the day of the funeral. Led by the new king, the cortège set out, crossed the Nile, and reached the eternal resting place. In front of the entrance they took leave of the deceased. The young king – or, in his absence, the priest Sem – touched the eyes and mouth with an adze and chisel to restore them to life. And then the lid was laid on top, the sarcophagus was lowered into the vault, and the dead pharaoh was left to his new existence.

But Ramses had not yet done enough for a father whom he had greatly loved. He had already ordered two statues of the king from the best sculptors in Thebes and Memphis. Now he embarked on the royal ship, taking a whole fleet with him, and journeyed north. His immediate purpose was to enter the Abydos canal and lay his offerings before Onnophris (Osiris). He saw, to his regret, that the buildings set up by former kings were now in a deplorable condition. Since their owners had ascended to heaven, the plans had been abandoned, because there had been no son to restore his father's monuments. The temple of Menmare (Seti I) had not been treated any better. There were statues of the king lying on the ground, and the frontier marks were not in place. The king summoned his counsellors, and explained his ambitious plans; having won their complete approval, he put them into execution. He chose architects, masons and engravers. They began to sculpt the statue of the year I, and arrangements were made to administer all the late king's property. Then King Ramses addressed a long speech to his father. We shall summarise the essentials:

I give thee the peoples of the South, who are bringing gifts for thy temple, and the peoples of the North, who are bringing tributes to thy noble countenance . . . I have magnified thy treasure, filling it with possessions in accordance with thy desires . . . I give thee a transport ship with its cargo on the sea. The merchants are trading their merchandise and their gold and silver and copperware . . . I give thee barges with their crews, and the carpenters are working so that there shall be an unceasing procession of boats to thy temple . . . I have set up the temple with every art and craft . . .

Behold, thou hast entered heaven, thou art with Re, mingling with the stars and with the Moon. Thou hast thy rest in the world below as its inhabitants rest beside Onnofris, master of eternity . . . When Re rises in the heaven, thy eyes are fixed on his beauty, when Atum [the sun of night] comes out of the world below [?], thou goest with him . . . Thou art one with the divine Enneade of the necropolis. Behold, I demand air for thy august nostrils, I proclaim thy name often every day . . . Thou shalt be as if thou wert still living while I reign. I have watched over thy temple

A fallen colossal head of Ramses II.

daily . . . My heart surrounds thee with solicitude, and I maintain the memory of thy name, while thou art in the world below. All shalt go well for thee, as long as I live, as long as Ramses endowed with life like Re shall endure.[6]

King Menmare, in the other world, understood every word of this speech, and answered at once, as a father on earth would answer his son. Ramses understood his reply perfectly well, and he transcribed it at the end of the dedicatory inscription of the temple of Abydos:

May your heart rejoice greatly, beloved son . . . Re grants you millions of years, eternity on the throne of Horus of living men. Osiris asks for thee the length of days of the heaven, in which you rise like Re every morning . . . I have said to Re with a loving heart: grant him eternity on earth as you granted it to Khepri . . . And when I entered the presence of Osiris, I repeated to him: Renew for him the length of days of thy son Horus . . . All the gods attend thee.

And Seti ended:

Thou comest as Re to men. The South and the North are beneath thy feet, imploring jubilees for Usimare-Setpenre and the length of days of the Master of the World when he rises and goes to rest, eternally and for ever.[7]

Before Ramses left the nome of the Great Land, he had the first prophet of Onuris (his capital near Abydos) presented to him; this was Nebunenef, whom he had resolved to raise to the dignity of high priest of Amun. The king still remembered the difficulties which had arisen between the monarchy and the priests of the most powerful of the gods, and he wanted to give himself every guarantee. He therefore named the prophets and the great dignitaries, but Amun only declared himself satisfied at the name of Nebunenef. Then the king gave him two golden rings and his canes and sent a royal messenger to inform the whole of Egypt that the house of Amun was allotted to him with his possessions and people.[8]

It was a fortunate choice, and no cloud overshadowed the relations of the monarchy and the clergy for the rest of the reign.

Ramses had now accomplished all his duties towards his father, both in Thebes and at Abydos. There was nothing now to keep him in the south. Once again he embarked on his ship, and the royal fleet set out for Memphis; here it paused for a while, and then entered a tributary of the Nile, the water of Avaris.

All along the Nile there were residential palaces where the king could make a brief stay, if he so wanted; but Ramses provided himself for long and frequent stays in a city of the North – or, rather, a city of the eastern Delta – which was the cradle of his family. He thus avoided being near the high priests of Amun, who were always disposed to lay down the law to the king; he avoided too the heat of the summer in Thebes, and perhaps he also avoided the bans which were imposed in Thebes. No one in the Delta residence forbade Ramses to drink the wine of Koenkemi, a wine sweeter than honey. He dreamed of creating a company of gods in his future dwelling-place; in this heavenly company, Amun, Set, Ptah and Harakhti would be equal and cease their quarrelling, and the divinities of neighbouring lands, Anta and Hurun, would be free to enter. Ramses was happy to think that this residence would be one of his titles to glory, but no doubt a stronger reason than this determined his choice. At the end of dynasty XVIII, the Hittite power had already clashed with Egypt; Seti I had managed to capture Kadesh, and had erected a stela on the banks of the Orontes; the upper part of it has been discovered.

Ramses certainly received alarming reports from his envoys about the plans of the one king who could challenge his hegemony. That is why he dreamed of building a stronghold quite a distance from the frontier; it would be a residence for him, and a place where he could assemble and train his archers and charioteers quite safely.

The reasons which had led the Hyksos to choose to live in Avaris were still valid in the time of Ramses II. The most cogent reason was the facility of communications with the Mediterranean, the Red Sea and the countries of the south. East of the old city of Avaris there began the land of Goshen: the Hyksos kings in Avaris had granted it to the Children of Israel when they had been authorised to live in Egypt. Having recaptured this city, the kings of dynasty XVIII did not trouble about these nomads, who for several years had let their flocks graze between the Pelusiac tributary of the Nile and the Wady Tumilat. The nomads did not worry anyone. But all this changed when the pharaoh came and settled on the country with a swarm of scribes and courtiers and soldiers. A new city had to rise from the desert and the ruins. Architects, masons and cutters of stone were not lacking in the workrooms, but there was a chance that there might be too little unskilled labour for the humbler tasks, dragging stones and moulding bricks, and it was then that people noticed the presence of the Children of Israel.

A census was taken of them at once. They were enlisted by scribes of their own nationality who were working themselves for Egyptian scribes, and they were forced to do the most arduous work, not only at Ramses's residence but at Pi-Tum, a city of the eastern Harpon. The Israelites bore their misfortune with patience, and, as they knew that Ramses had a heavy hand, they abstained from any protest during his lifetime.

And so the lettered men of the day praised Ramses' residence in poetic terms:

I arrived at Pi-Ramesse-miamun [wrote the scribe Pabas], and I found it in perfect condition. It is a noble and peerless domain, after the fashion of Thebes. Re himself founded this delightful residence.

What a joy to live there! Everything one could wish for, great and small, is there. Come, let us feast in its honour – let us have the feast of heaven and of the beginnings of the season.

How fortunate the day of thy life, how pleasant thy voice when thou didst ordain the building of Pi-Ramesse-miamun, a marvel for every foreign land, the uttermost point of Egypt, the building beautiful with balconies, lapis-lazuli and turquoise, the place where the cavalry are instructed, where infantry are assembled, the resting-place of thy archers, and of thy ships which bring thee tributes.[9]

Ramses' new residence had natural charm, and every kind of facility for the subjects, including that of approaching the sovereign and the great, which was certainly impossible at Thebes. There were perpetual feasts. All these advantages were appreciated by the many subjects who had wanted to stay close to the sun.

Even if we combine the statements of texts and the discoveries of archaeologists, it is difficult to form an exact idea of the Northern residence at the time of its foundation. It was so often devastated, restored, and again destroyed, that few stones, stelae or statues remain in their original places. The sandstone and black granite statues and the rose granite bas-reliefs must have acquired a new and extraordinary impressiveness against the black basalt flagstones. There were probably as many temples as divinities, some ten or so. The royal palace was enriched with gold and lapis-lazuli, and with all the stones known to the ancients; and, no doubt, as and when the royal family increased, new palaces were added to the first. Then came the work-rooms, the dwellings of the great functionaries, and beyond them the barracks and the stables. The whole surpassed the Ramesseum and Medinet Habu and was only surpassed by Karnak, on which so many centuries had left their mark. Foreign princes must have been dazzled by the riches of Ramses.

It was the beginning of Ramses' reign which saw the war with the Hittites, and this was the great event of the period.

Early in the month of May in the year 5, Ramses, followed by his guard, passed the fortress of Tjel, near Kantara, an obligatory route for any army going to or from Syria. A month later, he found himself in the Djahi. He had been preceded there by three detachments of troops. One was under the patronage of Amun, the second under Re, and the third was under Ptah; the troops had taken up position on the Phoenician coast. The soldiers were impressed by the beauty of the countryside, and the freshness and purity of the water; and, probably on the king's orders, they had engraved three stelae, two of which can still be seen, near the mouth of the river which the Romans called Lycus. A little further north, Ramses was able to meet Ahirem, king of Byblos; traces have been found of his passage in this friendly city. His intention was to go on north, along the coast, to Simyra, then perhaps to turn east, and follow the route which Thutmose III had taken a century earlier, in the other direction.

Ramses continued his way north, and reached the city of Ramses in the

Statue of Ramses II with a small figure of his favourite queen, Nofretari.
(*overleaf*) Head of Merenptah, long thought to have been the pharaoh of the Exodus.
(*overleaf right*) The other-worldly character of Osiris is emphasised by the use of green.

valley of the Pine, no doubt the valley of the Eleuthere. He went on to the Kadesh region in good spirits, for two Bedouin (Shosu) had just tricked him into believing that the 'vile fallen man of Khatti' was afraid of meeting the pharaoh, and was even now hiding in the Khaleb (Aleppo) region north of Tunip. The other contingents of troops went up into the Lebanon, for, as Ramses observes, the soldiers followed tracks as easily as they followed the causeways of Egypt.

When the drama was about to occur, Ramses, his guard and the Amun contingent found themselves north-west of Kadesh. The army of Re was fording the Orontes at Shabtuna, one iter (roughly nine miles and a half) from the place where Ramses had halted. The army of Ptah was further south at Irnam, and a fourth, the army of Set, was trying to catch up with the main column.

The engravers have given us an entirely peaceful impression of Ramses' camp. It is a vast square protected by a palisade of bucklers, or of objects shaped like bucklers. The king is sitting on a throne in front of his tent. His lion is tethered to an archway by one of its paws, and it lies sprawled out in a doze. The horses have been unharnessed to allow them to drink, and the asses are rolling in the dust, kicking or galloping.

Suddenly, three events occurred almost simultaneously, which brought Ramses back abruptly to real life. Hittites had broken down part of the palisade and had begun to loot; the Hittite army had attacked the army of Re while it was crossing the Orontes, and they had inflicted casualties on it. And finally Egyptian soldiers had captured a patrol sent out by the 'vile fallen man of Khatti'. Two men were led into Ramses's presence, and since the cudgel is an infallible means of ensuring speech, they confessed: 'We belong to the King of Khatti, and he has sent us to find out where His Majesty is.' – 'Where is the vile fallen man of Khatti? I have been told he is in the land of Khaleb, to the north of Khatti.' – 'Behold, the "vile fallen man of Khatti" comes with the many nations who are with him. They are more numerous than the grains of sand in the desert. Behold, they are ready to fight round the ancient city of Kadesh.' Ramses burst out in a fury, and he did not spare his officers. The vizier was despatched to collect the stragglers. In the face of this great peril, His Majesty rose up like Monthu. He put on his cuirass and seized his weapons. When his equerry, Mena, saw his master threatened by so many enemies, he began to tremble. Courage failed him, and terror overcame him. He said to His Majesty: 'O my good lord, valiant sovereign, great protector of Egypt, behold we are alone in the midst of our enemies. The soldiers and their chariots have abandoned us. How canst thou save them? You see that we are guiltless. Save us, Usimare.'

It was at this moment, or a little later, that the king made his touching appeal: 'What is it, O my father Amun? Does the father know his son no more?' And Ramses recalled all the proofs of his piety. The king's appeal was heard as far away as Unu in the South (the left bank of Thebes), and

Wall-painting on the inner chamber of the tomb of Inherkhau at Thebes; he stands in adoration before the *bennu*, the sacred heron which symbolised the soul of Osiris and was worshipped at Heliopolis as the sun god Re.

Ramses II receiving spies captured in the battle of Kadesh, from one of the reliefs at Abu Simbel.

immediately Ramses felt that Amun was worth more than hundreds of thousands of soldiers, more than millions of chariots. The Hittite king had deployed two thousand five hundred chariots in a long line which was meant to encircle Ramses and his followers, but the royal guard had also taken up their combat stations opposite the Hittite charioteers. Their armour was designed to resist attack by enemy chariots, and their round casques protected them against sword thrusts; the bucklers allowed them to ward off or blind the horses and then to finish them off with their fearsome swords.

The king, who was in the midst of his guard, set a fine example of self-command:

He shot arrows to his right, he defended himself on his left. The two thousand five hundred enemy chariots and their horses were overthrown. The enemy no longer had hands with which to fight and defend themselves. They could no longer draw or hold their swords. The vile king of Khatti, who was there in the midst of his soldiers and chariots in the fight against His Majesty, turned away from him trembling. The allies were astounded by the valour of the pharaoh, and cried: 'Every man for himself!', and beat the retreat. His Majesty pursued them like the griffon.

As usual, the king attributed this astonishing reversal of the situation to the valour of his arm alone.

Now that the battle was won, the armies of Re, Ptah and Set arrived on the scene, and he overwhelmed them with sarcasm.

None of you were there . . . None of you rose to help me while I was fighting . . . None of you came so that you could recount your exploits in the land of Egypt . . . The foreigners who have seen me [the Sherden] will repeat my name even to the most distant, unknown lands . . . I will give no reward to any of you, for you abandoned me, you left me alone in the face of my enemies. . . .

Next morning the 'vile fallen man of Khatti' sent a messenger with a letter which was nothing less than a demand for peace, drawn up in the humblest terms:

'Thou art Sutekh, Baal in person. The fear of thee is a fire in the land of the Khatti . . . Thy servant here speaks to thee and tells thee that thou art the son of Re in person. He has given thee all his lands joined together in one. The land of Kemi, the land of Khatti, behold they are in thy service . . . Is it well to kill thy servants? . . . Behold, thou didst kill them yesterday. Thou hast killed millions of them . . . Thou shalt leave no inheritance. Do not scatter thy property, mighty king, glorious in battle. Grant us breath.'

Then His Majesty hastened to summon the first among his army and charioteers, and his noblemen, and he told them of the request which the vile king of Khatti had made. They said without hesitation, and with one voice: 'Peace is a good thing, an excellent thing, our Sovereign and Master.' It was a heartfelt cry. Then they corrected themselves and said: 'There is no harm in peace, if thou makest peace. Who will greet thee in the day of thy wrath?'

The king listened to the counsels of wisdom. The enemy chariots had been broken by the guard, but the Egyptian army was not much inclined to assault the Hittite army which was strongly entrenched in Kadesh. It departed peacefully towards the South without even trying to capture the fortress, though everyone had seen the towers across the Orontes. The gods and goddesses, it was said, protected the army on its march. The king, great in victories, went on in peace, and entered Egypt at Pi-Ramesse, and rested in his palace of life and health like Re in his Akhet. The gods came to greet him and said: 'He is come, he is come, our beloved son Usimare-Setpenre son of Re Ramessu. They have granted him millions of jubilees on the throne of Re. All the lands of the world have prostrated themselves beneath his sandals for ever and ever.'

Ramses soon had a poetic account of his victory composed for him – indeed, it was an epic account, for the miraculous plays a large part in it – and he had it engraved in a place of honour in the finest of the temples, together with a simpler account, the bulletin and various episodes of the campaign. This collection of records is worthy of the event.[10]

And yet Syria was not to have peace again. In the year 8, Ramses appeared there in person, and hostilities occurred in one place or another nearly every year. Finally, in the year 21, Ramses and King Khattusilis decided to put an end to the wars by concluding a treaty. We are fortunate enough to have two versions: the Egyptian version, engraved on the walls of Karnak, and the Hittite version, discovered in the archives of the Hittite capital, Boghazkoy. 'The year 21, the 1st of the month of winter, the 21st, His Majesty was in the city of Pi-Ramesse. The two sovereigns, treating on a footing of equality, decided to establish a lasting peace between them.'[11]

Even after this treaty there were occasional clashes and bloodshed. Ramses was determined to keep a closer watch on his enemies and had set up a watch-tower on the road to Syria, under the protection of four divinities: Amun, Set, Astarte and Puadjit. Four statues represented the king: Ramesse-miamun shown here as god, Monthu in the two lands as herald, Sun of the Princes as Vizier, and Charm of Egypt as prince. This watch-tower had not passed unobserved by the king of Khatti, who sent word to the king of Kode:

Foreign captives depicted on the pedestal of a colossal statue at Abu Simbel. Their position beneath the pharaoh's feet emphasises their subjugation.

Prepare to hasten into Egypt. We shall say that the Souls of the god have shown themselves. We shall return thanks to Usimare so that he gives us the breath of his love. No land exists but for his love. May the Khatti be with his Souls. If he is alone, the god receives his offerings no more, and he sees the water of heaven no more. And so he will be with the Souls of Usimare, the bull which loves the brave.[12]

Every year, so Ramses claimed, the king of Khatti sent letters to appease him, but he refused to listen. Now when they saw their country in this deplorable situation, under the empire of the Great Souls of the Master of the Two Lands, the great chief of Khatti said to his army and his leading men:

What has come to pass? Our country is laid waste, our master Sutekh is angry with us, the heavens no longer give us water . . .

Let us strip ourselves of all our possessions, first among them my eldest daughter, and let us bear our gifts of honour to the perfect god so that he may give us peace and we may live.

And then he had his eldest daughter brought before him, with precious offerings of gold, silver, many curious objects and countless chariot horses, oxen and goats, thousands of sheep – everything that their country produced.

And they came to tell Ramses, saying:

'Here indeed is the great chief of Khatti bringing his eldest daughter and every kind of produce from his land . . . They are crossing impassable mountains, crossing treacherous gorges. They are approaching Your Majesty's frontiers. Send soldiers and great men to receive them.'

His Majesty smiled. The palace was full of joy to learn of this excellent event, the like of which had never been known in Egypt. He sent the army and the great men to hasten to meet the arrivals.

Now His Majesty deliberated in his own heart about the army:

'What is the situation of these people I have sent? They are going on a mission to Syria in these wintry days of rain and snow.'

And then he presented a great offering to his father Sutekh . . . The sky cleared; summer days arrived . . . As for the soldiers, they all rejoiced, and their hearts swelled with joy . . . They reached the residence of Ramses in the year 36, the 3rd month of the winter.

They brought the daughter of the great chief of Khatti, who had made the journey to Egypt to meet His Majesty. She was followed by the most splendid gifts . . . Now His Majesty saw that she was beautiful of countenance . . . She was agreeable to the heart of His Majesty, and he loved her above all things. He gave her a name: the king's wife: Manefrure [she who sees the beauty of Re] may she live.

Henceforward, when a man or woman went on a mission to Asia, they entered the land of Khatti without fear.[13] And so a princely marriage brought a happy end to a conflict which had long caused bloodshed to both countries.

Ramses certainly had many other wives before and after the Hittite princess; Nofretari, for instance, who often figures beside him. The Little Temple of Abu Simbel is dedicated to her as well as to the goddess Hathor.

(overleaf) Colossal figures flanking the portal to the Nofretari Temple at Abu Simbel. This small temple was dedicated by Ramses II to his queen and the goddess Hathor. Nofretari stands on the right next to a figure of the Pharaoh.

Ramses was very proud of his many children and has left us several lists of them. The most copious list includes no fewer than one hundred and sixty-two names; indeed one wonders if the grandchildren are listed as well as the children. We shall only mention Prince Khaemwise, who left a reputation as a scholar with a passion for old scriptures (he restored the pyramid of Unis); Merenptah, who succeeded Ramses, and Bant-Anta, the daughter of Anta, who was often mentioned and represented beside her father.

However important Asian affairs may have been in the time of Ramses, they could not distract his attention from the southern lands, where the Egyptians had so many interests. They received ebony and ivory from them, and skins and incense; gold-mines were exploited in the desert, though this was done with great difficulty.

There is much gold [people said], in the land of Ikita [to the east of the Second Cataract], but the way to it is extremely hard because of the lack of water. When prospectors go there to wash the gold, only half of them arrive. The others die of thirst on the way, with the asses who go ahead of them. The water in their leather bottles is not enough for their needs, either going or coming back. We can therefore bring back no more gold from these lands because there is no water.

According to a report of the royal son of Cush, kings had long ago tried to dig wells, but without success. Ramses' father, Menmare, who had been so successful east of Edfu, had been no more fortunate than the rest. He had undertaken to dig a well of a hundred cubits, but it had been left unfinished without any sign of water. This failure did not discourage Ramses' engineers: early in his reign, convinced that Hapi, father of the gods, would not fail to support his beloved son, they resumed the work, and this time succeeded. The water in the Duat (the subterranean world) obeyed the king and rose up in the well. Miners no longer died on the way to Ikita.[14]

The architects who were ordered to raise temples on the bank of the Nile found themselves confronted with a great problem. There was very little space between the river and the foot of the cliff. Whenever possible, they built the outposts open to the air. This was the case at Beit el Ouly and at Gerf Hussein, and again at Wady Es-Sebua, but the temple of Derr is entirely underground.

Other kings had preceded Ramses in these particular places. He wanted to have a site which was his alone, and he chose the cliff of Abu Simbel which falls almost sheer to the Nile. He had four colossi carved in the sandstone mountain. Sixty feet high, they sat with their hands on their laps and their backs to a high, blank wall; this was simply decorated with a hieroglyphic band, a cornice with palms, and a frieze of crouching baboons. The colossi faced the river, keeping a fixed watch on the eastern bank and the tracks which led to the gold mines. Their features were grave and noble, the nose large and arched, the lower lip slightly protruding. The face was no longer that of the youthful Ramses of the Turin Museum and the bas-relief at Tanis:

it was the king in his prime, as he was when he signed the peace treaty with the Hittites.

The entrance door, surmounted by an image of Harmakhis in a niche, separates the two pairs of colossi. The interior goes back for a hundred and sixty-five feet and is divided into several rooms. The ceiling in the first room is supported by eight other colossi: these represent Ramses, standing, and metamorphosed into Osiris. When the rising sun shines into the grotto, it awakens these eight mighty images, and under its warm caress they seem to smile, giving them a moment's life. Nowhere has Egyptian art expressed the power of Re, the devotion of his faithful, with such grandeur. Happy the travellers who have admired this masterpiece in the place which Ramses and his architects once gave it.

At Thebes, there are monuments which attest the glory of Ramses: the Ramesseum on the left bank; the Pylon of Luxor, and, above all, the hypostyle room of the great temple of Karnak. In the presence of this forest of pillars, as in the presence of the pyramids, the visitor is petrified with wonder. It is quite true, as Champollion said, that no other people, ancient or modern, has conceived architecture on such a gigantic scale.

(*overleaf*) Two column heads in Ramses' temple, showing the carvings on them.
(*below*) The columns of Seti I and Ramses II in the temple of Amun at Karnak.

This last work was done at the same time as the works already mentioned and those we still have to mention as we go down the Nile: the works at Abydos, and in every city of any importance, but above all in Memphis, Heliopolis, Pi-Ramesse and many cities of the Delta. But these monuments have been so pitilessly exploited by the limeburners that they have been reduced to a few stones.

Perhaps Ramses took more interest in the sculptors than he did in the other gifted men of his time. In the year 8 of his reign he visited the quarries of the Red Mountain near Heliopolis, where he discovered a colossal block of stone, ready to be sculpted. He had a stele engraved and put up in the temple of Hathor, and on this stele he declared the interest he took in everyone who helped to sculpt the sphinxes, and the upright, seated, and kneeling statues with which he peopled the temples of Egypt.

Take heed of my words: Here are your possessions. Reality proves what I say. It is I, Ramses, who create the generations and make them live. Food and drink are before you, and there is nothing to be desired. I improve your way of life so that you work for me with love, and I am fortified by your hopes of success. Ample provisions are given you, so that you will live to fulfil your task . . . There are granaries of wheat so that you do not pass a day without food. You are each paid for a month . . .

For you I have filled the shops with all sorts of things, pastry and meat and cake to feed you; sandals, clothes, and divers perfumes to anoint your heads every ten days, so that you may be dressed all the year round, so that you should wear good shoes every day, so that none among you spends the night in fear of want . . . I have ordered men to feed you even in the years of famine, and people of the marshes to bring you fish and fowl. Ships sail for you from North to South, bringing barley, starch and wheat, salt and beans without end.

I have done all this, saying: 'As long as you live you will want likewise to work for me'.

We cannot even begin to count the statues. In Thebes alone they are innumerable, giants sixty feet high (at the Ramesseum), colossi standing or sitting, or groups of the king with a deity or with one of his wives. But I cannot refrain from pointing out one or two masterpieces. The seated statue in the Turin Museum (number 1380) is so well preserved that it seems to have come straight from a studio. The silhouette is elegant and the features are extremely delicate. The expression is benign, the modelling of the cheeks is perfect, the nose long and thin, as it is on the bas-reliefs of the early years of his reign. Statuette number 42142 in Cairo comes from the favissa; it shows the king dragging himself along on his knees and pushing an offering before him, in a movement of extraordinary grace. As for the two colossi of Memphis (the smaller one has recently been put up in a square in Cairo), they do not deserve to be called masterpieces, but they are both very good works. The big one in fine limestone is quite remarkable and seems to be a perfect reproduction of the gentle features of the king.

The hypostyle room of Ramses II's funerary temple – the Ramesseum – at Thebes.

Grey granite statue from Tanis showing Ramses II protected by the goddess Anta.

(*opposite*) Part of a colossal statue of Ramses II from his temple at Luxor, showing the tiny carving of his wife Nefertari.

Carving of Nofretari on the façade of the Great Temple at Abu Simbel.

(*opposite above*) Bas-relief of a Nile god from the temple of Hathor, Abu Simbel.
(*opposite below*) Wall-painting of female attendants from Queen Nofretari's tomb at Thebes.

Pi-Ramesse, the king's favourite residence, was a veritable Ramses museum. The inhabitants of the royal palace could contemplate four granite giants sixty feet high, whose names we already know; then a number of colossi fifteen to twenty feet high, and usually made of sandstone. We know seven of these, but there used to be more. The features are conventional, but the modelling is often admirable. Ramses is nearly always accompanied by a princess; Bant-Anta, perhaps, or the Hittite princess, clasping the leg of her mighty husband. Then come the triads, Ramses holding the deities by the hand, and the dyades, the king beside a goddess. The triads are extremely curious. The three figures are connected by the large slab which they are leaning on. The face is triangular and much larger than life. One remarkably ingenious sculptor executed a sort of rebus. The subject was Ramses, seated, and protected by a falcon god (Hurun). Ramses the child (*ma*) is wearing the disc (*Re*) and holding the plant of the South (*sw*). All of which gives Ramessu. Finally there are other statues, representing Ramses alone, rather larger than life. They show careful workmanship, but (were it not for the inscriptions) the excessive size of the face would prevent us from recognising the king. However, we can clearly recognise Ramses on the obelisks, the mural bas-reliefs and the stelae.

It seems that Ramses' great concern, in the second part of his life, was the preparation for jubilees. The first was celebrated in the year 36, the eighth (and last to our knowledge) in the year 52. The first jubilees were certainly celebrated at Pi-Ramesse. We have discovered the lintel and columns of the granite temple which the king erected for it. From this time onwards, he ceased to appear on battlefields, settling down to lead a peaceful life among his children and his favourite artists.

Vandals have not spared the tomb which Ramses had planned for himself in the Valley of Kings (number 7). They have stripped the mummy of all its ornaments, and taken it out of its gilt coffin. The wooden coffin in which it was then laid came to rest, after several moves, in the royal burial-place at Der el-Bahri, and finally at the Cairo Museum. It measures 5 ft 8 ins from head to foot. The forehead is low and narrow, the nose is long, thin and arched; the jaw is strong and powerful, and the lips are thick. The mummy's face gives quite a good idea of the king's face in the last years of his life. The expression is not very intelligent but the mummy has kept an air of majesty which has somehow survived the grotesque embalming. It was a very different Ramses who, in his prime, greeted the Hittite princess: then his features expressed pride, nobility and benevolence.

Ramses deserved to be called great. He proved his remarkable courage at the battle of Kadesh, and became legendary even in his lifetime. Throughout his life he was conscientious in the exercise of his kingship. His monstrous egoism was tempered by a kindness of heart which was appreciated by his soldiers, his artists, his family, and, one may even say, by all his subjects.

(*opposite left*) The mummy of Ramses II.
(*opposite right*) The pink granite sarcophagus of Merenptah.

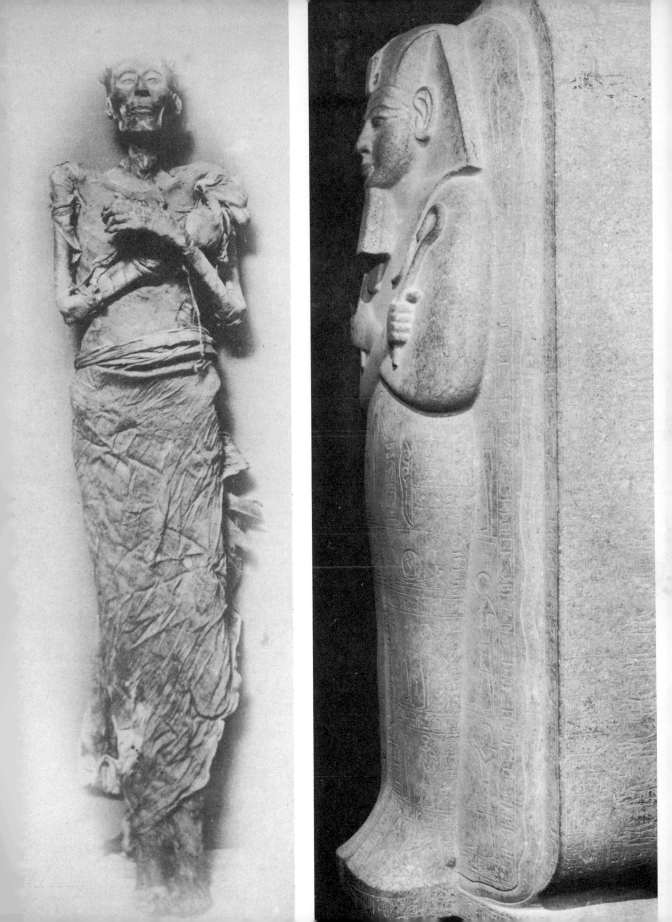

The Valley of Kings in the western Theban mountains.

Merenptah, the king of the Exodus

Merenptah is fourteenth in the list of the sons of Ramses II and was his successor. There were therefore a good dozen princes between himself and the throne, but there is no proof that he did anything to promote himself. His mother Isinofre had been the mother of Prince Khaemwise and Princess Bant-Anta. We do not know how old Merenptah was when he ascended to the throne, but in any case he was no longer young. He was an old man succeeding another old man. His mummy was found in the chamber of the tomb of Amenhotep II, which had been turned into a royal burial-place, and its face suggests that cunning was the dominant feature of his character. One may compare the mummy with the two recumbent likenesses of Merenptah on the lids of his sarcophagi: the real sarcophagus from the Valley of Kings, and the sarcophagus from the cenotaph which he had had built in the cemetery (Kher) planned by his father at Pi-Ramesse. There is no doubt that, by giving their model an expression both paternal and cunning, the sculptors caught his likeness. Merenptah inherited a long nose from his father and grandfather, but he had none of the truly royal quality which Seti and Ramses show in their faces.

In Merenptah's time, the danger to Egypt did not come from the north-east, but from the west. The western peoples, the Tjehnyu and Tjemeh, had more than once given Egypt cause for anxiety. It had been only recently that Ramses II had been obliged to intervene against them, as we see on a magnificent bas-relief from the temple of Abu Simbel.

There are many records, enamelled plaques, paintings and bas-reliefs, which give us an idea of these people. They have pointed beards, aquiline noses, and a thick lock of hair hanging over the left cheek. Their arms and legs are tattooed, and over their waist-cloth and head-band they wear a multicoloured cloak which is open in front and only covers the left shoulder. In Merenptah's time their chief, Maraye, had gathered the established inhabitants of the country and certain immigrants under his command: the Akawasha (who must be the Achaeans); the Tursha, the Luka, the Sheklesh (who may have given their name to Sicily), and finally the Sherden (the Egyptians knew these people well, having enrolled whole battalions of them in the royal guard). This coalition did not merely dream of extorting a tribute or province from the Egyptians, but of transporting themselves and their arms and baggage into the Valley of the Nile and living there happily like the Hyksos before them. At the beginning of the year 5 they set out on their march, occupying the western nomes almost unopposed. Their real objective was Memphis, but to deceive the Egyptians they crossed the Nile and made their way towards the nomes of the East. They camped outside Bilbeis and on the banks of the Ity canal, which waters Heliopolis and Bubastis before it disappears into a lake near the nome of Soped. Perhaps they divided their forces in two, with half of them going back up the western tributary of the Nile with Memphis as their objective. The other half hoped to provoke a general uprising in Palestine, which the Children of Israel would join, thus justifying the fears which the Bible attributes to the pharaoh (Ramses ii): 'Behold the Children of Israel are stronger and more numerous than we are. Let us look to them for fear that they should multiply, that they should join our enemies and war against us and go up again from this country.'

Merenptah assembled his officers, and explained the danger to them, asserting his right to lead his troops into battle. It was a noble claim, but it seemed to many that the sexagenarian king was making a foolish mistake, inviting death even. Ptah his patron took pity on him. He appeared to him in his sleep, and enjoined him to keep calm and to have confidence. – 'Send forth your foot soldiers, send charioteers without number to attack the borders of Pi-yer.' We know nothing about Pi-yer, although it was doubtless well within the Delta. The battle lasted six hours, and ended with the rout of the invaders. Maraye lost his treasure, his armour, and his women, and had to flee in shame. More than seven thousand of the enemy lay dead on the battle-field. An equal number of prisoners was distributed among the soldiers. The return to Thebes was a triumph.[1]

The news of this almost miraculous victory soon reached the lands of the East. Their warriors had been ready to join the Libyans and take part in the looting, but these fine plans were abandoned, and no one thought of any-thing, now, except peace. This is what we read at the end of the stele called the stele of Israel:

> No one raised his head among the Nine Arches.
> Tjehnyu is subdued,
> Khatti is in peace,
> Canaan is captured with all that is wicked therein,
> Ashkelon is transported,
> Gezer has been seized,
> Yenoam is as if it were not,
> Israel is razed to the ground, and has no more seed. Khor is as a widow [kharet] of Egypt.[2]

In this unique record, Israel is associated geographically with the peoples of Palestine, and chronologically with the year 5 of Merenptah. The Children of Israel had been informed of what was in preparation in Libya and left Egypt in a body just as the pharaoh was stripping the eastern frontier of troops in order to face the double Libyan threat.

We may summarise the facts as follows. The Children of Israel learned of the death of the king who had reduced them to servitude, and they uttered a cry of relief. They had a leader Moses, and since the pharaoh lived in Pi-Ramesse, on the border of the land of Goshen where the Israelites lived, Moses

Statue from an official's tomb at Thebes dating from dynasty XIX.

had only to take a step to be in the presence of the pharaoh: anyone at Pi-Ramesse could appear before the king and lay his petition before him. Moses therefore claimed for his people the right to go into the wilderness and serve their God. The pharaoh refused. Then came the first of the plagues, the frogs. The pharaoh was impressed at first, but soon hardened his heart, and from then on he was relentless to the end. For he was in a good position to know that the so-called plagues – the epidemics, murrains, grasshoppers, hail and darkness, etc – were just calamities which often befell Egypt, without the least supernatural intervention ... The day the Children of Israel left Egypt, they did not take the road of the Philistines, although it was near, because they knew that there were Egyptian strongholds all along it as far as Hebron. They took the road to the Sea of Rushes (Yam Suphi); this was not so well guarded, for it was known that slaves had managed to escape by way of Tjeku (Pi-Tum).

It is hard to give an exact location for the Sea of Rushes, but almost certainly it is the same as the Bitter Lakes. As for the stages of the Exodus, our uncertainty about them is due to the fact that the biblical indications are approximate – Succothi, Pi-Hariroth – and to the fact that there are several migdols in the region.

Archaeologists have looked for Baal-Zephon near a stela on which there was some mention of Baal, but their researches have yielded nothing definite. It is only certain that the Egyptians did not pursue the Children of Israel for long, and that they found themselves safe in the wilderness.

It has been accepted, without any proof, that after his victory over the Libyans, Merenptah undertook a Palestinian campaign. Actually this is most uncertain. The Israel stele simply records a factual statement. The people who expected to join in the Egyptian attack were careful not to move when they learned of the Libyan disaster, and Merenptah has his own explanation for this. After the year 5, Merenptah could erect statues in peace, and raise monuments at Pi-Ramesse, Thebes and Gebel Silsilah to celebrate the feasts of the Nile in Nubia.

Merenptah had married one of his sisters, Isinofre, who bore the same name as his mother. He had a son by her, Prince Sety-Merenptah, who succeeded him as King Seti II.

In due course Merenptah prepared a funerary temple for himself on the left bank of the Nile, and it was in its ruins that Flinders Petrie found the stele of Israel. Economically, the king had had it engraved on the obverse of a great stela of Amenhotep III (Cairo 34025). His tomb in the Valley of Kings is near the tomb of Ramses III. The great pink granite sarcophagus is still in place in the main chamber. On the lid, which is shaped like a cartouche, rests the body of the king.

The gateway of the precinct of Ramses III's mortuary temple at Medinet Habu. The guardian statue portrays the lion-headed goddess, Sekhmet.

Despite the triumph of his troops over the Libyan invaders, Merenptah would be one of the most insignificant pharaohs in history if he had not happened to be at Pi-Ramesse when the Children of Israel were trying to leave Egypt. The account of the Exodus can in no way be considered an historical document. All the same, the chronicler who made Moses' interlocutor an impressionable, cunning, superstitious yet stubborn man may have come near the truth. He has certainly recreated the atmosphere of those discussions, at the end of which the Children of Israel left Egypt. They had lived there for four centuries before setting out on their great adventure.

Ramses III embraced by the goddess
Isis, whose hand and shoulder are
painted in the paler flesh-colour used in
reliefs to denote women and goddesses.

6   A time of conflicts

Ramses III, the last of the great pharaohs

The beginning of dynasty XIX had been brilliant under Ramses I and Seti I, and Ramses II had raised it to great heights of power and glory. But it seems to have ended in a rather miserable manner. We know little about the order and length of the reigns of the last sovereigns. The legitimate kings were displaced by Arsu, a usurper of Syrian origin who brought back the worst days of the Hyksos era. The whole country was under his rule, and no one thought of anything except robbing and killing his neighbour. The gods were treated no better than humankind and received no more offerings in their temples. But they decided to correct this state of things, and to do so with vigour. They established their son as the king of their choice, to reign over all the land in their stead: King Usikhaure Setpenre, beloved of Amun, the son of Re, Setnakhte who loves Re, beloved of Amun, Life, Health, Strength. 'He was like Khopri, like Set in his anger.' He restored order throughout the land and compelled people to forget their quarrels and become friends. He re-established the temples as they had been, with offerings for the Enneade of the gods.

Just as the saviour king at the beginning of dynasty XVIII had been called Seti, so the new sovereign was called Nakhte-Seti (Seti is strong). His reign was brief. His wife was a Princess Tiye Merenese, and he was buried in the tomb of Queen Twosre. Their son was Ramses III, who reigned for thirty-two years and composed his titulary as follows:

> Horus: Valiant bull great in royalty.
> Vulture-Cobra: Strong and valiant like his father Monthu [there are many variants of this].
> Golden Horus: Rich in years like Ptah, sovereign who protects Egypt and chastises the foreigners.
> King of the South and North: Usimare Meramun, the son of Re Ramessu Hekaon.

Relief from the pink granite sarcophagus of Ramses III.

Ramses III died in the thirty-second year of his reign, but we do not know how old he was when he ascended the throne. Like Ramses II, whom he took as his example in all things, he enlarged his official titulary by multiple epithets, most of which designate him as an all-conquering hero.

Ramses III, who so admired Ramses II, was far from having the impressive physique of Seti I, or the charm of Ramses II in his youth. The few statues there are of him give him a round head and a broad, heavy face.[1] The expression lacks nobility. There is no doubt that Ramses III liked women and delighted in having naked girls to serve him with perfumes and delicacies. He used to chuck them under the chin, in a genial way. And yet perhaps he preferred his horses: he took great care of them and used to go and see them in their stables. He wore his state costume for these visits and carried a very long cane and a whip. Behind him came umbrella-bearers, holding the ostrich-feather parasol high above his head, and duty officers, carrying provisions and gold plate. Sentinels had already caught sight of the procession, and now they sounded the king's fanfare. There were eight horses, pawing the ground at their master's approach. Apparently the stable-boys had already prepared to set them loose, and perhaps they were set free to canter around.[2]

We must remember that the Egyptians did not ride horses separately, like their enemies; they harnessed them in pairs to a two-wheeled chariot. The charioteer and a single warrior stood on the platform.

Before the king went to war, he reviewed his army and attended the distribution of weapons. There were Sherden among the foot-soldiers, as there had been in the days of Ramses II, and from time to time, after successful battles, they would be joined by captured Philistines, Libyans and Syrians. These foreigners kept their own national weapons in the Egyptian army. Ramses III took his place on a dais with a balcony; then, leaning on a cushion, he listened to his officers' speeches, and said: 'Let them bring the weapons for all to see. With these weapons, and the courage of my father Amun, we shall humble the rebel lands which know not Egypt.' The weapons were laid out in categories. Here were the helmets: they covered the head well, and they were made with a visor and two cords. Beside them were the triangular bows, the sheaves of arrows, the coats-of-mail, and the long-handled, scythe-shaped swords. Most of these weapons were Syrian in origin. In fact the Egyptians had beaten their enemies with their own weapons.[3]

Prince Mesher belonged to a new Libyan tribe (the Meshwesh had reduced the former inhabitants of the land of Tjehnyu into submission). In the year 11 he decided to attack Egypt. He advanced towards Memphis but was completely defeated, and countless prisoners were left in Egyptian hands. Mesher, wounded by the king himself, was captured by the Egyptians, his horses had been pulled down, and his equerry killed. Mesher turned to the pharaoh, and raising his arms, and holding up his forefinger, admitted his defeat. Keper,

Wall-painting showing the Egyptian two-wheeled chariot, which was drawn by a pair of horses and was used both for hunting and warfare.

the Libyan king, came in person to find Ramses III, asking to suffer the torture in his stead, but Ramses was inexorable. Mesher was killed with great ceremony, and then Keper was given his turn.[4] I do not know how Ramses II would have behaved on this occasion. The captives were reduced to slavery, the men enlisted, the women and children enrolled among the servants of the temples. The soldiers surrendered in whole groups. They held their long vertical lances like candles and stretched out their left hands, palm downwards. Ramses III could write of the Libyans:

They had their seat in Egypt, for they had taken the cities on the Western side from Hikuptah [Memphis] to Keroben [situation unknown]. They had reached the bank of the great current [the Rosetta tributary], they had taken possession of the local cities, and the oxen, for a great number of years. They were in Egypt. But I destroyed them, I slaughtered them all . . . I forced them to go back across the Egyptian frontier. I brought home the rest like some vast booty, spurring them on, collecting them like fowl before my horses, their women and children in thousands, and their cattle in millions. I enlisted their princes. I marked them as slaves, sealed with my name.[5]

Before he had even finished with the Libyans, Ramses III had to face an invasion from the opposite direction. The sea peoples may have come from far away, but they had reached the Syrian coast and were coming down it to Egypt, by sea and land. The Peleset, for example, had piled up women, children and provisions in solid-wheeled carts drawn by four oxen.[6] Their long ships were rather like the Egyptian ones. They themselves were great hulks of men, and their crowns of feathers made them seem even more enormous and formidable. With these Peleset were other tribes, also sea people: the Weshwesh (formerly unknown), the Tjekker and the Sheklesh, not to mention a new wave of Sherden which had not yet been assimilated. (The Peleset ended their migration by settling in Egypt; but the other peoples, who were driven out of Egypt, continued their course as far as the western Mediterranean.) The battle was terrible. The Egyptians shot at the enemy ships which had come too close inshore, sending clouds of arrows down on to them and pursuing them in their own ships. They then boarded the enemy craft. Egypt had once again escaped a formidable invasion.[7]

After these two hard lessons, the Libyans and the sea peoples were completely cured of Egyptian ambitions. The Egyptian soldiers (the national troops and the foreign mercenaries), the Sherden and the Kehek, returned to their quarters, and slept in peace, fearing neither Nubian nor Syrian. Their weapons and bows were stacked in the stores. They themselves lacked nothing, and they had their children with them.[8] The king was with them too, to safeguard and protect them. From time to time the old warrior instinct got the upper hand, and in the presence of the pharaoh, the princes and officers, even in the presence of foreign visitors, there were combats quite as hard as those described by the epic poets of Greece and Rome. Egyptians, Libyans and Nubians gave each other formidable blows.

When Ramses III set out for the hunt, he was always accompanied by a numerous suite. It was fortunate that he was. One day some lions hurled themselves at his chariot. A wounded lion tried to claw out the arrow from its breast. Another, hit by two arrows and a javelin, went and lay down in the reeds. There was a third lion, which was still dangerous, but the king had time to turn on it, and give it its death-blow.[9] On another occasion, the royal party came across a herd of wild bulls near a marsh. One bull was pierced by arrows and fell on its back, beating the air with its hooves. Another bull rolled under the horses' hooves. A third bull, its tail stiff with the effort, its tongue hanging out, tried, with a desperate bound, to reach the water, but fell exhausted on its knees.[10] Compared with these absorbing hunts, the pursuit of the antelope was a mere game, and the king enjoyed it alone in the desert.

The desert so attracted the Egyptians that Ramses III had formed

Ramses III shown hunting desert game (*above*) and wild bulls in the marshes (*below*), from the First Pylon in the mortuary temple at Medinet Habu.

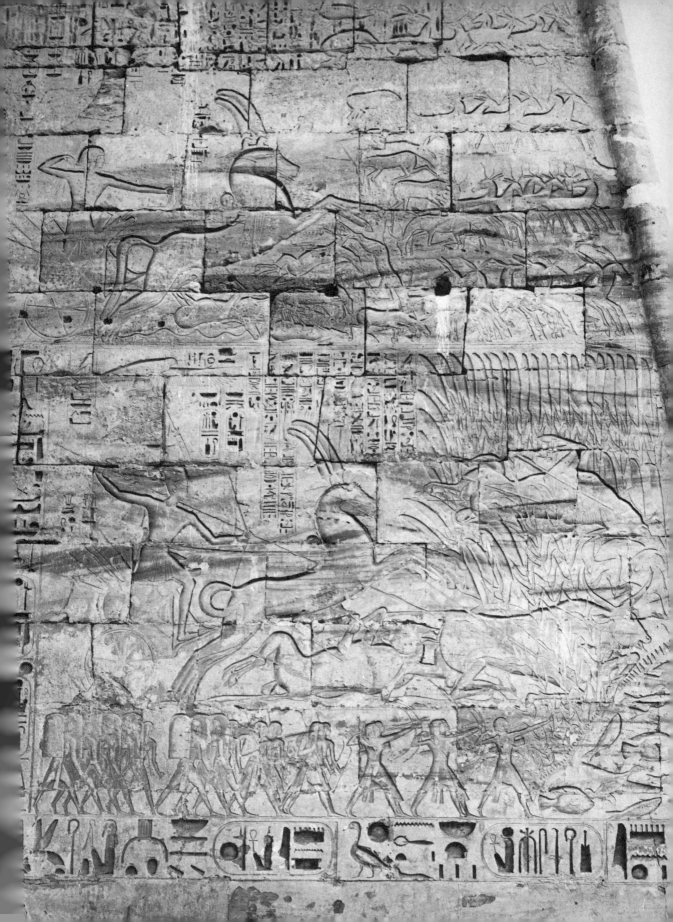

companies of archers at Memphis and Heliopolis. They escorted the explorers of the eastern desert, who sought for rare products: resin from the turpentine-tree (*sonter*), and wild honey. In fact they were killing two birds with one stone, for in some parts of the desert it was the turpentine-trees which attracted the bees. It was the same men who uprooted turpentine plants and replanted them in the temple gardens.[11]

There was something which the gods appreciated even more than the resin of the turpentine-trees, and this was incense, when it was burned in front of their statues. The Egyptians had been bringing incense from Punt for so long that by now they had a perfect knowledge of the land and sea routes which led to the incense country. ('I have built great *menechou*,' writes Ramses III; 'they are preceded by *bair* with large crews, and men to escort them.') The chief archers were attached to the *menechou*, and so were the assistants, who loaded them with countless things from Egypt. It seems that new types of ship had now replaced the *kebenit* of Queen Hatshepsut's day. These *menechou* were preceded by scouts. But what follows in Ramses' narrative is particularly surprising. 'They left the great sea of Muqed. They reached the mountain of Punt without serious loss, safe and sound because of the fear that I inspired.' Muqed is the name of the Euphrates. Unless the scribe is wrong, the sea of Muqed must be the Persian Gulf. For want of a more explicit text, one must presume that the pinewood planks and beams were dragged across Syria to the Euphrates, as in the days of Thutmose III. And so they must have built *menechous* and *bairs* which went down the river and round the enormous Arabian peninsula. When they had reached their destination, the Egyptian ships were laden with the produce of To-neter, the marvels of their mountains, the dry incense of Punt – more incense than they could measure. The children of the chiefs of To-neter walked in front of their produce, and they took the land route to Egypt. When they left the land of Punt, the ships took the sea route again, while the caravans formed up and finally reached Thebes. There was a splendid ceremony when the ships and the caravans arrived together. They ended their journey with festivities, and presented their produce as if it was a marvel. 'The princes' children came to greet me,' Ramses recorded, 'to kiss the ground and prostrate themselves before me. I gave them to the Enneade of all the gods of this land, so as to calm their leaders in the morning.'[12]

The jubilee in the year 30 was one of the last events of the reign. In principle, it should have been celebrated at Memphis, since Ptah was the lord of jubilees, but Ramses II had already chosen his city of Pi-Ramesse for this ceremony, and had built jubilee palaces there. Ramses III followed his example, and there were immense preparations several years in advance. The king had already had the temple of Ptah restored in the year 22. In the year 29 the vizier To, governor of the city of El Kab and the nome of the Rural, had received orders to return the sacred barges to the goddess Nekhabit, so as to celebrate the Sed festival, and to accomplish her rites in the jubilee temples.

They reached Pi-Ramesse, the great *ka* of Pra, in the year 29 and it was the king himself who grasped the prow of the sacred barge. All the chief cities of the nome made similar preparations, and for several weeks a motley crowd invaded the walks and avenues of the palace, and countless barges were moored along the quays.[13]

A warrior king like Ramses III could not fail to be a builder as well. He needed the vast surfaces of pylons and long walls to show the world his victories over the enemies of Egypt, the hunts in which he had exposed himself to danger, the acts of piety with which he had thanked the gods for their constant protection. Of all the monuments which he erected over the length and breadth of Egypt, there is one which eclipses and summarises everything, and that is the group on the left bank of the Nile at Medinet Habu. It is not only a temple for Amun and for the king, it is a residence, a palace and a stronghold. The group is heralded by a building of which there is now no other example in Egypt; it is copied from the Syrian strongholds which Ramses III had so often attacked and occupied. There were similar buildings in the region of the Isthmus of Suez, and they are mentioned in the texts. The migdol of Medinet Habu consists of two high towers, one on either side of a narrow courtyard. Seven princes, in chains, represent the peoples of the North: Khatti, Aamu, Zakari, Sherden, Sheklesh, Tursha and Peleset. On the consoles, decorated with the figures of prisoners-of-war, there used to be statues of the king. From the upper storeys you have a magnificent view of the great temple, and you can still share Ramses' pleasure, and rest there with pretty women.

About eighty yards to the west there stands the great temple with its two pylons, its courtyards, its hypostyle rooms and its chambers. The bas-reliefs record all the events of a very active reign: war in Libya and Syria, the attempted attack by the sea peoples, the lion and wild bull hunts, the episodes of the feast of Min which coincided with the king's own feast, not to mention the calendar of feasts and many other scenes.

All the buildings which Ramses had recently built, and those which he had restored and embellished, were richly endowed, and we have the details of this royal munificence in a splendid document called the great Harris Papyrus. This is all the more exhaustive since it was drawn up when Ramses was already an inhabitant of the other world.[14]

It is King Ramses III, the great god, who speaks, exalting his father, the venerable god Amun Re Sonter, he who existed before every god or goddess, he who engendered himself . . . 'Lend me thy ears, master of gods, hearken to my prayers . . . Thou hast established me in the place of my father, as thou hast established Horus in the place of Osiris . . . I have not oppressed, I have not stolen the place of another. I have not transgressed against any of thy commands . . . I have multiplied lasting and numerous benefits for thee . . . .'

Then comes the list of these benefits, first among them Medinet Habu.

However, this vast munificence was not shown without a certain ulterior motive. It was also an investment. The king was thinking of himself, of his posthumous life, and, above all, of his son:

Make my son appear as king in the dwelling of Tum, perfect him as a valiant bull . . . Ramses sovereign of truth . . . Thou didst proclaim him king when he was a young man. Thou dost set him over men as sovereign of the lands. Give him a royalty of millions of years . . . Thou art the shield which protects him every day. Let his sword and mace be over the Asiatics, let them be overthrown by his fear like Baal . . . Let him enlarge his frontiers as he wills . . . May the love of him be in the heart of the gods and goddesses, the sweetness of him, the veneration of him in the heart of Payt. It is thou who makest him live. Settle his royalty on his son's son. Grant that the Nile will be great and strong in his time, to feed his royalty with abundant food. Grant that the kings who know not Egypt may bow down before thy sacred palace.

(*left*) Slaves from a relief in the temple at Medinet Habu.

(*opposite*) Column and statue in the peristyle of Ramses III's temple at Karnak.

Alabaster head of the goddess Hathor in the guise of a cow, from Der el-Bahri.

Then came the turn of Harakhti and Tum, of Iutixas and Hathor, the gods of Heliopolis. These four were far from attaining the wealth of the Theban triad, but they need not be pitied. The king had renewed their temple and their precincts and their rules; they could show the visitor an *uadja* in gold, lapis and turquoise, and a golden boat. The sacred lakes had been cleaned. The vast gardens were made beautiful with trees and plants. An olive plantation allowed the flames to rise inside the palace, and an aviary gathered in the inhabitants of the air. A special body of huntsmen was formed to bring in honey and terebinth from the desert, and capture the oryx, whose sacrifice was most pleasing to the gods. There were also great barges set aside for their service . . .

At the end of the great Harris Papyrus, Ramses III repeated what he had said at the beginning. He recalled, even more clearly, that he had reached the west like Osiris:

Hearken to my prayer . . . Establish my son as king, he will govern the two lands in his fashion . . . As thou dost appear on earth with Horus and the two women, so establish thou the white crown and the divine double crown . . . Protect my son, guard all his limbs, strengthen his bones. Make his span on earth like that of Sekhmet and Soped . . . Give him the Nine Bows joined together beneath his feet, may they implore peace in thy name . . . Thou didst create him when he was young. Thou didst name him prince on the double throne of Geb. Thy prophecy has come to pass. Grant him a great royalty increased by great jubilees like Tatjenen.

Memphis, the third great religious centre, was the domain of Ptah Sekhmet, Nefertum and the Enneade of the gods of Hikuptah.

I am thy son whom thou hast caused to ascend into the place of thy father in peace. I am inspired by thy counsels. Thou didst multiply thy kindnesses to me when I was on earth. Ramses has not been ungrateful to the lord of the jubilees. He has created his companies of huntsmen to gather honey and terebinth in the eastern desert, he has built a vessel of a hundred and thirty cubits, and he has commanded a series of original things, a great golden dresser [*hnt*], inkwells, enamelled vases and other objects for the cult. He has embellished the court of the temple of the Wall of Soped with plantations of terebinth and incense-trees.

And so Ramses comes to the end of an abundant list, but he does not forget his beloved son:

May his length of days be beautiful on earth, may it pass among cries of joy . . . Grant that he shall triumph for Egypt as sovereign of the two lands. He will be deified before thee under thy praises, for he has enlarged the frontiers [an example of perfect prophecy]. The Nine Arches and the lands will acclaim him. Grant that life and length of life may be joined in his flesh, grant him health in his limbs in every season.

After the three religious capitals there were the sanctuaries of the gods which had to be remembered. They were gathered into a single chapter: Anukis, Thoth at Khmun, Osiris at Abydos, Wepwawet at Asyut, Set at Nebet, Hor-Khentamenty at Athribis, Set at Pi-Ramesse; and there were others, too, less powerful, perhaps, but Ramses pleaded his son's cause to them with the same ardour he had shown to the mighty gods: 'Give him Egypt so that his heart may blossom under the acclamations and that it may be united beneath his sandals for eternity.' The last thought of the aged king concerned his beloved son. No one did as much as Ramses III to ensure the future of his monarchy, and no one found a more direct and sincere tone in which to do so. No doubt he had good reason for that. He was afraid of seeing another plot like that which had ended his own reign.

As Queen Isis was the great royal wife, her eldest son was chosen as hereditary prince, and his younger brothers after him. A princess called Tiye decided that if they got rid of the old king and the sons of Isis, nothing would prevent her own son, called Pentawere, from ascending the throne. Two palace functionaries agreed to recruit partisans for her, and to rouse opinion against the king. (At the time of the trial they received the derisory names of

Ramses III mourned by the goddesses
Isis and Nephthys.

(*left*) Painted relief from the Osiris chapel of Seti II at Abydos, showing Seti in the
guise of Osiris with the ibis-headed god Thoth.

Paibekkamen, 'the blind servant', and Mesedsure, 'Re detests him'.) It seems quite certain that, when the trial began, Ramses III, who had appointed the jury and given them full powers, was no longer among the living. 'And now,' he is recorded as saying at the beginning of the preliminary speech, 'now I tell you in all truth what has happened and about those who have committed this crime. I do this so that the crime of which they are guilty will return on their own heads. As for me, I am protected and defended for ever and ever, for I am among the vindicated kings who stand before Amun-Re, king of the gods, and Osiris, master of eternity.'

The culprits were arrested, not only the four we have mentioned, but also ten officials and six women. The four chief culprits expiated their crime, but the inquiry still dragged on. Two members of the tribunal and an officer of the bodyguard abandoned the counsel of perfection: they learned that some women had escaped, and went to meet them in a place of ill renown. This time, however, they were discovered by people who were in earnest, and they had their ears and noses cut off for a start. As for the accused, they were summoned one after the other. They gave their names and heard the evidence against them. The court proclaimed them guilty and pronounced the sentence; it was nearly always sentence of death. 'They were put in their places (perhaps on the site of their tombs), and they died by their own hand,' that is to say they were forced to commit suicide. There was no mercy for those who had attacked the pharaoh.[15]

It is a curious thing that the most important documents for the study of the reign were drawn up in accordance with the king's wishes but after his death.

Ramses III had had his tomb dug and decorated in the Valley of the Kings; it has long been called the tomb of the Harpist, because of the magnificent musician who is playing a harp as large as himself, in the presence of Harakhte. Chamber number 6 has been called 'The King's Treasure', because of the representations of weapons and various objects, many of which are exotic. This may be why Ramses III has had a reputation for being immensely wealthy. We shall come back to this. The king's sarcophagus has been divided between the Fitzwilliam Museum, which has the lid, and the Louvre, which has the trough. The mummy was found, wrapped up in its bands, in the burial-place at Der el-Bahri, but the wooden coffin ended up, no one knows how, in the burial-place of Amenhotep II.

Was Ramses III a great king? He had succeeded to an impoverished Egypt, invaded in the west by the Libyans, threatened in the north-east by the sea peoples and the Syrians. He managed to ward off these dangers, and though he did not equal Ramses II in his splendour, or in the number of his buildings, he found the means, in a reign of some thirty years, of executing one of the handsomest, best-preserved buildings in Egypt. The great Harris Papyrus attests his piety, his munificence to the gods, and, above all, his paternal love. I believe that no king found such convincing accents in which to draw the

(*opposite above*) Head of the silver mummy-case of Psusennes I, found in his tomb at Tanis, enclosed in the granite sarcophagus.
(*opposite below*) Gilded mask of Psusennes I found by the author at Tanis in 1940.

attention of the supreme gods to his heir. We may note, in his favour, that he liked horses, trees and gardens, but he was certainly cruel when he refused to pardon the Libyan prince. He put trees and gardens everywhere; during his reign all the temples were surrounded with green. Good and evil mingled in him, but the good seemed to prevail, and he did not merit the plot which ended his reign.

Several distinguished modern scholars have identified Ramses III with Rampsinite, the hero in a story of some brigands which is told by Herodotus (II, 121). Rampsinite means Ramses son of Neit. No such epithet has yet been found. It is possible, for in any city the king is theoretically the son of the local god or goddess. For the moment, the only argument that one can adduce is the king's vast fortune; this gave him the idea of building a well-concealed treasury. Ramses III had in fact built treasure-houses for precious things alongside every temple of the first importance. However, the rest of the story belongs to legend.

Psusennes, a king of Tanis

The events which Ramses III had feared for his son did not occur at once. For half a century, from Ramses IV to Ramses IX, the peace was not disturbed at home or abroad. It was in the year 15 of Ramses IX that bandits first attacked a royal tomb.

The pillaging of tombs soon became quite general, and the government did not really bother to stop it until there was nothing – or almost nothing – left to steal. The depredation was terrible. The mummies of the great pharaohs had to be taken out of their tombs and put, without finery or jewels, into simple wooden coffins; these were piled up in the royal burial-place at Der el-Bahri, and in a chamber in the tomb of Amenhotep II. But these odious deeds were only the symptom – or the result – of much more serious troubles which were bathing Egypt in blood: the War of the Unclean. In the time of Ramses II and Ramses III, the king's prestige had imposed religious peace; but it is probable that Set, the principal god of the North, and Amun, the great god of Thebes, were only waiting for a favourable occasion to engage in a merciless struggle for supremacy.

I shall not describe this war, which I have discussed elsewhere.[1] The Setians were the stronger at first, but the Thebans took heart, conquered the country and completely rid it of Set and his allies. This Theban victory was not achieved without great destruction, which took place largely at the

Gold mummy-mask of Sheshonk II, from the antechamber of the tomb of Psusennes I, found by the author in 1939. The eyebrows and eyes had been inlaid in a different material.

(*left*) Sistrum with the head of the goddess Hathor: this, the most sacred instrument used in temple services, was only held by high ranking women.

(*below*) Ushabti of Henutowe, Psusennes' wife; these statuettes deputised for the deceased when forced labour was required in the next world.

expense of Set. When the war ended, Pi-Ramesse, the superb residence which could have lasted for centuries, was only a heap of ruins. Another result of the war was that the last Ramses, the eleventh, lost his throne, even though he had fought on the winning side. For six years there was no pharaoh at all. This interval has been called the renewal of births. And so we reach the year 1035, and we find not one pharaoh, but two kings: one, Smendes, reigning over the Delta, and the other, Hrihor, High Priest of Amun, master of Upper Egypt. Smendes, to judge by his name, must have been a man from Mendes. He installed himself as best he could on the ruins of Pi-Ramesse, and henceforward the city was called Tanis. He maintained good relations with Hrihor, and together they organised the expedition which brought Wenamun to the shores of Syria, and finally to Byblos. Here King Tjikarbaal showed him that the weak are always in the wrong. Smendes married Mutnodjme; this Mutnodjme was, I believe, a descendant of Ramses, which means that Psusennes himself belonged to the glorious family of Ramses.[2] The reign of King Psusennes must have begun about 1055. It was certainly quite long: forty years according to the most conservative estimate, forty-six according to another.

Psusennes' titles are as complete as those of the greatest pharaohs:

Horus: He belongs to the valiant Bull, given by Amun, a wealthy [king] who appears in Thebes.
Vulture-Cobra: He is great in monuments at Ipet-Esut [Karnak].
Golden Horus: He unites the lands, and masters the Nine Bows.
King: Here Psusennes hesitates between Akheperre-setsenamun and a title: First Prophet of Amun.

Finally came his personal name, meaning 'the light which rises from the city'.

All these titles, especially that of the First Prophet of Amun, bring us back to Upper Egypt. Even Psusennes' personal name, 'the light which rises from the city', may be interpreted in two different ways: Thebes, the queen of cities, is the city *par excellence*, but Tanis is another Thebes. In fact, Psusennes' power hardly went beyond Lower Egypt.

According to Psusennes' names, he had the strength of a thousand lions and a thousand panthers. He was the taker of cities. Two of his military leaders had the honour of sharing his tomb with him. It is more surprising to find that he maintained relations with the commercial centre which sent lapis-lazuli all over the world. He had a great deal of lapis-lazuli and he made much use of it. There is a lapis-lazuli ball which bears a finely engraved inscription in cuneiform characters; it mentions the lady Napalte, daughter of the grand vizier Ibach-Ilu, who recommends her to the gods Enlil and Ninlil of the city of Enlil in Mesopotamia near Assur. This lady was probably one of Psusennes' wives; she it was who gave him the handsome necklet of which the pearl with the cuneiforms was the finest ornament.

Psusennes also had some Egyptian wives. We know of two: the worshipper of Hathor, Hentitowe, and Isemkheb. Hentitowe bears the title of mother of the child Chons, which almost certainly means that she gave the king an hereditary prince. Hentitowe also had a daughter, Makare, who left for Thebes accompanied by her mother, and equipped with a long decree signed by her father. Once in Thebes, she became the divine worshipper of Amun, and later the wife of the high priest of Amun, Pinudjem. She died very young, having given birth to a daughter. Her double coffin, her shroud, her mummy, her papyrus and her funerary statuettes are preserved in the royal burial-place at Der el-Bahri. Her mother, who had come with her, accomplished several pious works in Thebes and attended her daughter's enthronement as divine worshipper. Perhaps she returned to Tanis, but she died in Thebes.

The name of Isemkheb recalls the sojourn of Isis and the child Horus in the marshes of the Delta. We know hardly anything about her, except that she was a royal daughter. After the death of his first wife, Pinudjem took for his wife another daughter of Psusennes. She was a high priestess of Amun, and she was called Henutowe.

The division of Egypt into two kingdoms had therefore not raised up the South against the North. The king of Tanis and the high priest of Amun were on the best possible terms, and even Pinudjem managed to share the kingship with Psusennes. He had a title, Imy-ta, 'he who is in earth', which relates him to the god of the nome of the Cuisse in the Delta. At the end of his life, Psusennes had another associate, Neferkare Amenemsut: a fragment of his tomb has revealed his existence and function to us.

Now that Egypt was no longer a great power, now that she had given up all her conquests, all her people seemed to have taken refuge in piety. They had banished Set from Egypt. His temple had been destroyed, and his name and image has been defaced. All devotion was now given to the Theban triad, who had established themselves in Tanis as if it was their own domain. Perhaps Chons was the favourite among them, but the secondary deities were not forgotten; among them was a Libyan goddess by the name of Chahedet.

Psusennes certainly spent the greater part of his reign at Tanis. He had found the city in a sad state, and as the ancient walls had almost crumbled away, he began by building a new wall. This alone was a colossal work, for it was anything from thirty to forty-five feet thick. Its layout was extremely strange: it was an irregular, six-sided quadrilateral. From the building of this wall we can date some of the foundation sacrifices which our mission found under the bricks and in the embrasures of gates under the sand. They consist of a pottery jar containing the skeleton of a child and another skeleton which lies outstretched beside it. The Bible gives us the best commentary on these sacrifices. Hiel the Bethelite, it is said in I Kings, XVI, 34, laid the foundation of Jericho on Abiram, his eldest son, and set up the gates on his youngest son, Segub. In the light of this text we can maintain that one of the sacrifices was made in connection with the wall and the second with the gate; but nothing indicates the identity of the victims. It is strange, to say the least, that a king who used the names of Amun and the Theban triad should have practised this barbaric custom – there are further examples of it in Tanis. All the bricks are stamped with Psusennes' second name, who must have considered the wall as something sacred.

This wall was much smaller than the other walls of Tanis, but it was still vast enough to contain the temples, the palace, and the site which had been reserved for the tomb. The temple was built on the cheap with materials from the temples of Ramses. The fine granite blocks have been coated with lime-stone, thick enough for figures and inscriptions to be engraved on them. The temple has been completely destroyed, but we know the site exactly, thanks to a foundation deposit which was found intact in the great temple, fifteen yards from the axis. This deposit allows us to place a second one to the north of the axis (this was certainly discovered by Mariette, who did not record its location), and we can also place the two others. Psusennes' temple could hardly have measured more than thirty by fifty yards. There was another temple near the jubilee palaces of Ramses II which was built entirely of fine white limestone, most carefully engraved. What remains does not give us much idea of the decorations. The gods were clearly the three Theban gods who had taken possession of Ramses' domain.

Even under Ramses III the sculpture of circular bosses and bas-reliefs was very inferior to what it had been in the days of the great king. The decline continued during the reign of the last of the Ramses; and the War of the Unclean, which caused the destruction of so many fine works, also, in all probability, brought the closing of the workshops. When order was established again, there were no longer any artists who could handle the chisel. Fortunately for Psusennes, the great Temple of Tanis was a museum of sculpture in which the only problem was one of choice. Ramses II had already helped himself very liberally. On the lions with human faces Psusennes has added his name to the names of the great king. He also took possession of two re-markable works which may not, until then, have been requisitioned. The first, an incontestable masterpiece, is the group of the two bearers of offerings, with their opulent beards and thick hair; they are advancing in step to present a table garnished with birds and fish and nenuphars. The other work is a group of baboons of which only one is more or less intact. The baboon is seated on a square base. It is beautifully done. The original inscriptions on the base have been erased and replaced by Psusennes. On the front we can read his titles, and on the sides everything is about one god, Chons. The baboon of Thoth may therefore also represent Chons, and Chons also has affinities with the god of Hermopolis. And so Psusennes furnished his temples with sculpture very cheaply.

Throughout Upper Egypt, the royal or private tombs are lined up against

(*left*) The reverse side of a scarab issued by Psusennes I.

(*left*) Gold, lotus shaped chalice found in the tomb of Psusennes.

(*opposite*) Gold falcon head from the sarcophagus of Sheshonk v, found in the tomb of Psusennes.

the great wall of the desert; but in the interior of the Delta, far from the desert, other solutions had to be found. Psusennes built his tomb inside the walls of Tanis, as near his temple and palace as possible. The personnel who attended to the palace and the temple also looked after the tomb, so that the dead men enjoyed the benefit of all that was done for the gods. Throughout Upper Egypt, the royal tombs and the tombs of the great functionaries were given majestic dimensions. Naturally there was no question of this at Tanis. Psusennes' tomb is a small building, measuring externally not more than sixty feet in length and fifteen feet in height. There is a central building in granite, its blocks are carefully matched and joined by bronze dovetails, and it is surrounded by a building in limestone. One descends to it through a well; then one crosses a passage to find oneself in an ante-chamber decorated with

The pink granite sarcophagus of Psusennes discovered by the author while working at Tanis in 1940.

bas-reliefs. This ante-chamber serves two chambers in the granite building, and a limestone chamber. Leading to the two granite chambers was a separate passage cut off by a granite stopper which had been put into place with bronze rollers; we brought it back into the ante-chamber by the same process. A window in the limestone chamber opened on to the ante-chamber. A fourth chamber, next to the first, had no windows. That makes four vaults in all. They were originally attributed to Psusennes, his mother and two of his companions-in-arms: Onkhefenmut, who was also a descendant of the Ramses, and Undebawended, a man of Mendes, like Psusennes' predecessor.

One great pink granite sarcophagus filled half the chamber of Psusennes. It had been removed from Merenptah's cenotaph at Pi-Ramesse. The king's body lay outstretched on the lid. A small goddess, the North Wind, knelt behind

Entrance to the tomb of Onkhefenmut found by the author.

him and freshened his face with her hands. There were a great many things in the first half of the room: a great sealed alabaster jar, four vases with emblematic heads for lids, a multitude of funerary statuettes; and above all, a wonderful collection of objects, sacred and profane, in gold, silver and bronze. There was a bronze stove which came from the jubilee palace of Ramses II. There were a golden carafe and goblets which had been used by the king when he went hunting or warring. Then there were family mementoes, to give the king the illusion that, even in his vault, he was still among his kindred. It is strange that, while sculpture on stone was neglected, the goldsmiths and jewellers worked as well as in the past.

The reverse of the coffin lid was decorated with a wonderful picture of Nut in a semicircular boss, escorted by the astral barges. In the vat was another sarcophagus, in black granite, which had also been usurped; this contained a silver coffin in which the mummy lay in all its finery. Nut stretched out her body over the king as if to intoxicate him with her beauty, and the king never tired of gazing at the goddess. For three thousand years in this stone prison the union of the dead king and the celestial goddess was consummated.

King Psusennes' intentions were only half respected. The royal vault was not touched: we found it intact when we entered it on 15 February 1940. The vault of Undebawended had been spared because no external sign gave away its existence; but Queen Mutnodjme's vault had been re-opened, its inscription had been partly defaced and the coffin taken out of the sarcophagus to make room for one of Psusennes' successors, who had a small, ill-protected tomb nearby. We do not know what happened to the queen. A similar substitution occurred in the vault of the royal son Onkhefenmut.

Psusennes' antechamber must have been richly furnished. It was converted into a royal burial-place in the course of dynasty XXII. Inside it we found a silver coffin with a falcon head. This coffin contained the richly apparelled mummy of King Hedjkheperre Sheshonk, who until then had been completely unknown. His place in dynasty XXII has been a subject of debate. The fine coffin was flanked by two gilt wooden coffins whose owners are unknown to us. We do not even know if they were placed there at the same time as Sheshonk. In all likelihood, the peace of the tomb had not been disturbed again until modern times, though thieves had made many soundings round it.

In the meanwhile, dynasty XXI continued its inglorious existence. It ended when a chief of Libyan origin overthrew its last representative, who was also called Psusennes.

7 The rule of foreigners

Sheshonk I, a Libyan king

From dynasty XXI to the time when Cambyses conquered it in 517 BC, Egypt was governed by kings of foreign origin: first by Libyans (dynasties XXII and XXIII), then by Ethiopians (dynasties XXIV and XXV), and finally by the princes of Sais who were Libyans again.

Outwardly, at least, these kings lived like the native sovereigns. They made no changes in the coronation and the jubilee, but we are not always sure where to find their tombs, and their faces are often unknown to us.

In the chapter on Ramses III, I emphasised the danger which the Libyans presented to Egypt. As the king himself had observed:

They had their seat in Egypt, having taken the cities on the western side from Hikuptah [Memphis] to Keroben [situation unknown]. They had reached the bank of the great river, from one end to the other. They had taken possession of the cities of the Oxen region [this was a commercial centre through which all the oxen imported from Libya had passed since time immemorial], and they had had them for a number of years. But I destroyed them, I massacred all of them together. I forced them to go back across the frontiers of Egypt. I brought back the rest like some great booty, spurring them on, gathering them like fowl before my horses; their women and children by the thousand, their cattle by the million. I enlisted their princes in my fortresses. I gave them chief archers, and tribal chiefs; I made them into slaves marked with my name, their women and children likewise. I presented their flocks at the temple of Amun.[1]

No doubt the Libyans were harshly treated if they fell into Egyptian hands in the time of Ramses III. But there were more peaceful arrangements too. It was the same Ramses III who declared that after his victories the Egyptian army, largely composed of foreigners, Sherden and Libyans, could rest in the delights of peace; the men lay stretched out on their backs, fearing neither Nubians nor Syrians, their weapons and bows stacked up in the stores, happy to have their wives and children near them.

It was easy to foresee the results of such policies. The former enemies of Egypt furnished the greater part of the army; it was not long before they

Bronze statue of Queen Karoma, Osorkon's wife, made for her chapel at Karnak. The details of the floral collar and embroidered dress were inlaid with gold, silver and electrum.

demanded and obtained leaders who were men of their own race. This was the case with the Meshwesh, who had been among the fiercest foes of Egypt under Ramses III.

Towards the end of dynasty XXI, they had a Sheshonk for their leader, then a Nemrat whose son was King Sheshonk, founder of dynasty XXII. The descendants of Sheshonk I were in turn called Nemrat, Osorkon and Takelot. These were semitic names, and Sheshonk himself recalls the god of Susa Susinak. This line was connected with another line of Libyan origin. Its founder was a Tjehnyu called Buyuwawa, 'may he take root again and again, may he be planted again and again, may he endure and endure, may he grow green in the temple of Herichef king of the two lands, sovereign of the two banks, unique son of man, unique, enduring for eternity in Ha-ninsu (Heracleopolis).' The sons of this founder were called Mawasata, Nebnechi and Paihuti (the Peasant), and they were succeeded by Sheshonk, husband of the royal mother Mehetemwaskhe, and Nemrat, husband of the divine mother Tentsepeh. This last couple were the parents of the future King Sheshonk.[2] These two women were amply provided with religious titles; they were also the daughters of a great chief of the Ma (an abbreviation of Meshwesh). Sheshonk, the son of Tentsepeh, had, therefore, no trouble in obtaining the title of great chief of the Ma, and since he had an army at his disposal, he easily ascended the throne on the death of the last Psusennes. Indeed, he may even have done so in the lifetime of Psusennes, who had become quite useless as a king. Sheshonk had taken care that his son Osorkon, who would succeed him some twenty years later, had married a Princess Makare, the daughter of Psusennes. We may therefore assume that the dynastic change took place without any trouble.

Sheshonk's titulary goes as follows:

> Horus: Valiant bull beloved of Re, whom he has caused to appear as king of the two lands.
> Vulture-Cobra: Double-crowned, like Horus son of Isis.
> Golden Horus: Most mighty, he who strikes the Nine Bows.
> King: Hedjkheperre Setpenre.
> Son of Re, Sheshonk sovereign of Onou.

Sheshonk's coronation took place at Heliopolis, and it was to Re, its god, that he first expressed his gratitude. His wife Karoma is mentioned on the Harpason stela, and the Berlin Museum has some *ouchebetis* and vases with her name, the origin of which is unknown. This is certainly the first time that the name appears. It was borne by other princesses; I do not know whether we must consider it as a Libyan name.

Sheshonk reigned for twenty-one years, after which he was succeeded by his son Osorkon I. This king is attested by a great stela found in the oasis of Dakhla, and another in the quarries of Gebel Silsilah; there are signs of him in the great temple at Karnak, and at Memphis, Pi-Tum and Tanis. He was therefore not boasting when he affirmed in his titulary that he was the king of the two lands. He was not a great builder. The portico known as the portico of the Bubastides at Karnak is due to his successors. He erected a great number of statues of Mut in the temple of Mut; they are now scattered among the museums of Europe.

At Tanis we discovered several very fine blocks of limestone: the remains of a monumental door. The complete titulary is engraved on the base of sphinx A 23 in the Louvre, which comes from Tanis. Sheshonk did not leave any statue of himself, and we have no idea of his physical type, or of his face, but we do have some idea of a number of his descendants: we know Osorkon I from his statue at Byblos, Sheshonk II from the gold mask on his mummy (undeniably semitic in character); we know Sheshonk III from the bas-reliefs on the monumental door, and those on his tomb. But that does not help us with Sheshonk I.

We come now to the great event of the reign of Sheshonk I. The Egyptians know it from the great picture on the external south wall at Karnak, in which Amun is presenting the king with a hundred and fifty-six cities taken from the Jews.[3] On the Palestine side, the affair is known from the relatively circumstantial account given in the Bible (1 Kings, XIV, 25–6). The bas-relief at Karnak is not dated. The biblical account is dated in the fifth year of the reign of Rehoboam, son of Solomon.

Various incidents had led up to the hostilities. During the reign of David, an Edomite prince, Hadad, had fled to Egypt with some servants to escape the general massacre which Joab had decreed. Hadad was still a small boy. The pharaoh gave him a house, promised him bread, and gave him some land. Soon Hadad had found grace in his sight. The pharaoh also gave him a wife, a sister of his own wife, the sister of the great lady Tahpenes. Hadad's son was brought up among the children of the pharaoh. Years went by, and Hadad learned that David had gone to rest with his fathers, and that Joab was dead. He said to the pharaoh: 'Let me depart from Egypt that I may go into my own land.' But the pharaoh said to him: 'What dost thou need with me that thou shouldst seek to go from me into thy land?' He answered: 'Nothing, but thou shouldst let me go.' And he departed, and reigned over Edom.

Soon afterwards, Solomon became the son-in-law of Pharaoh (1 Kings, III, 1 and IX, 16). The Bible does not indicate the name of the pharaoh, nor that of the princess. It does however tell us that the pharaoh had taken possession of Gezer, burning it down and killing the Canaanites living in the city. These events must have occurred under the last Psusennes, while the grandfather or father of King Sheshonk was great chief of the Ma.

When Sheshonk became king, he soon began hostilities against the king of Judea, because, says the Bible, he had transgressed against the Lord. He really did so in order to seize the fabulous treasures of Solomon, and, perhaps, because he had an old quarrel to settle.

In fact when Solomon sought to put Jeroboam to death, Jeroboam fled to Egypt, and there he remained until Solomon's death (1 Kings, XI, 40). This expedition was prepared very carefully, and I think we may connect it with the sending of a statuette to Abibaal, king of Byblos. This statuette is damaged but enough remains to show us that the king of Byblos had an inscription engraved round the king's two cartouches. This inscription, in alphabetic Phoenician, meant: '[Statue presented by] Abibaal, king of Byblos, soken of Byblos in Egypt, to the Lady of Byblos. May she prolong the days of Abibaal and his years over Byblos.' King Sheshonk proved by this gift that he considered Abibaal as his ally, and Byblos as a point of support. (Long ago the army of Ramses II had deployed itself on the Phoenician coast before he went into the Lebanon north and south of Byblos.) As for the king of Byblos, he used this statue as a palladium, in case Rehoboam should turn against him.

At last, in the fifth year of King Rehoboam, it came to pass that Sheshonk, king of Egypt, went up against Jerusalem, because they had transgressed against the Lord (II Chronicles, XII, 2–10). It is generally thought that this expedition took place towards the end of the reign of Sheshonk (about 930 BC), but there is no proof of this. Sheshonk had assembled some really formidable forces: twelve hundred chariots and sixty thousand horsemen. No one could count the multitude which had come with him from Egypt, but it included Libyans, Sukkiims and Ethiopians. Before I continue, I must emphasise how unexpected it is to find this mention of sixty thousand horsemen. Nothing on the Egyptian side confirms the existence of a body of horsemen in the Egyptian army. The presence of the Libyans and Ethiopians is quite natural, but the Sukkiims are not found anywhere else. However that may be, this veritable tide submerged Palestine. 'It captured the fortified cities in Judah and it reached Jerusalem. These fortified cities [archaeologists have found traces of them] made no resistance. The discovery of a stone with the name of Sheshonk in the ruins of Mutesallim, the ancient Megiddo, confirms the biblical and Egyptian statements.'[4] And so Sheshonk took the treasures of the house of the Lord and the treasures of the king's house. He took everything. Since he had taken the shields of gold which Solomon had made, King Rehoboam had shields of brass made in their place, and he committed them to the hands of the chief of the guard, who kept the entrance to the king's house. What did the king of Egypt do after his victory? No bulletin gives us any information. Probably his vast booty was collected together and despatched to Egypt, and, when this was done, the army made a triumphal return. Henceforward, Sheshonk only thought of commemorating his victory in a manner which was worthy of it.

In agreement with his son Iuput, the high priest of Amun, who had no doubt taken his place during the campaign, he sent the great chief of works,

Statuette in fine limestone found at Karnak, showing King Osorkon launching a sacred boat. This was most probably a votive gift made by the king to the temple on some festive occasion; traces of the original gilding and polychrome colour remain.

Landscape in the Sinai desert, scene of some of the pharaohs' battles.

Horemsaf, to Silsila, where people were quarrying sandstone – a fine building material. A new quarry was opened when King Sheshonk began work for the monuments to his father Amun-Re, master of the throne of the two lands, so that the god might grant him the jubilees of Re, 'the years of Tum living for ever'.[5] The king had worked out a great building programme. He wanted to build a stone pylon, and a hypostyle room for feasts, surrounded with columns. Circumstances decreed that his programme should not be carried out, and he contented himself with joining the south wall of the hypostyle room to the temple of Ramses III, and building the Bubastides portico further north. As for the commemorative picture of the Palestine campaign, it was sculpted on those parts of the wall of Seti I which were still undecorated. In his right hand, a gigantic Amun holds a scythe-shaped sword called Khepech; in his left hand he holds five ranks of places in Palestine bound together with cords. Each is figured by a crenellated cartouche containing its name,

(*opposite*) Mummy-case (cartonnage) of painted stucco, now in the Fitzwilliam Museum in Cambridge. The body seems to be enfolded by the protecting wings of bird-deities.

(*opposite*) A group of three gods, dating from the Twenty-second Dynasty.

(*right*) A painted coffin cover probably of the late Twenty-second Dynasty.

surmounted by a prisoner whose aquiline nose, prominent cheekbones and beard, indicate his semitic origin. The goddess of Thebes also leads five ranks of captives. On the right, the unfinished figure of the king brandishes a mace over still more prisoners.

The number of captured cities rose, in all, to one hundred and fifty-six, but Carchemish and Kadesh are not among them, nor are any of the distant cities conquered during dynasty XVIII. Jerusalem was found in the part which was lost, but there remain Megiddo and other cities. Egyptologists have found it hard to decipher their names from the barbaric orthography.

As for the treasures, we have some fine remnants of them. There is a pair of golden bracelets, with matching jewels, which Sheshonk II had slipped over his wrists; our mission found them in 1939, when it found the antechamber of Psusennes' tomb. We have no definite proof that these bracelets came from Palestine, but it remains highly likely: the two bracelets are virtually identical, and are composed of two unequal sections joined by hinges. The central motif of the small section is an *oudja* set on a basket. The larger section is decorated with alternate blue and gold bands. The two cartouches of King Sheshonk I are engraved inside.[6]

The king made no further expeditions. Either because of his age or his state of health he was left with only one subject for meditation, and this was his eternal resting-place. Osorkon I, however, attempted an expedition, but it ended in bloodshed and failure.

The resting-place of Sheshonk I remains an enigma, for if there is no positive proof that this tomb was built at Tanis, several fragments discovered in the tomb of Sheshonk III belong to the founder of dynasty XXII. There were two fragments of a vase, one of which was engraved with the name of Sheshonk I had not buried the unfortunate conqueror's mummy, for safety, it was stolen from us while I was putting our finds into order.[7]

To sum up: Osorkon II, Takelot II, Sheshonk II and Sheshonk III all had themselves buried at Tanis. The founder of the dynasty must have set the example, but his tomb was discovered by clandestine diggers, and nothing of it now remains except the fragments I have mentioned. Even these would not have fallen into our hands if the functionaries responsible for the tomb of Sheshonk I had not buried the unfortunate conqueror's mummy, for safety, in the tomb of Sheshonk III. In the same way, the mummy of Sheshonk II had been saved by those who had stored it in Psusennes' antechamber. But we must remember that archaeology lives on hopes, and we have not lost all hope of finding at least the site of the tomb of Sheshonk I.

Piankhy, a king of Napata

Piankhy's story was a prodigious one. King of Napata, master of Upper and Lower Nubia and of Southern Egypt, he rapidly conquered the whole of Egypt, and received the submission of all the princes who had divided the land of Kemi among themselves. Napata, his capital and his point of departure, is situated between the Third and Fourth Cataracts (rather nearer the Fourth). It was there that Mariette, and later Reisner, found some great historic stelae – including Piankhy's stela, which gives us abundant information about this long, unbroken progress. The city had been known to the Egyptians since Thutmose III, but neither this conqueror nor the other warrior pharaohs had extended their conquests towards the South. It was as if the Gebel Barkal had acted as a gigantic boundary.

Towards the end of dynasty XX, under the last Ramses, the Setians and their Palestinian allies had spread throughout Upper Egypt, sowing ruin and desolation everywhere. The chief of the soldiers of Amun had taken refuge south of Aswan, but thirteen years later Hrihor drove back all these barbarians – the Unclean, as they were called – beyond the frontiers. He was the last viceroy of Cush to be nominated by the pharaoh, and his son, who was called Payonkh, made his appearance as a royal son and soon as a king. He ruled over a kingdom which stretched from Aswan to Napata, and his descendants were only waiting for a favourable occasion to resume their march towards the North. They were to wait for this opportunity for nearly three centuries. At the moment when the account on Piankhy's stela begins, the Nubians were already masters of the whole Thebaid.[1] Piankhy took up Hrihor's unfulfilled ambitions as his own. A great stretch of time divides them, but the two men are so alike that we must accept Piankhy – his father and mother are unknown to Egyptologists – as a direct descendant of the last governor of Nubia to be nominated by the pharaoh.

Most cities along the Nile valley had a fortified wall around them and were able to resist an attack; but at this period there was more ingenuity and initiative among the besiegers than among the besieged. In fact the nomes of To-Chemua, north of Thebes, seemed an easy prey to Piankhy, and he found it hard to restrain the zeal of his troops.

At the other end of Egypt, however, there was another personage who cherished ambitions very like his own. This was Prince Tefnakhte, great chief of the Ma and prince of the West.[2] While Piankhy was enlarging his domains in a northerly direction, as far as Thebes, Tefnakhte had not wasted his time, and he now dominated the whole of the West as far as the nome of the White Wall and the city of Neter in the nome of the Divine Calf.

He continued his march towards the South with a massive army, and he brought the two lands together behind him. The princes, and the regents of palaces lay at his feet like greyhounds, as if they were the companions of his feet. No stronghold tried to resist him. Meidum and four cities of the West opened their gates because of him. And then he turned against the nomes of the East.

There were four successive strongholds on a narrow strip of the Nile Valley: Heboinu, near Minya, Teudjoi, the King's Castle and Chief of the Cow (the modern Atfih). Tefnakhte laid siege to Ha-ninsu (Heracleopolis), making it like a serpent with its tail in its mouth: he stopped those who wanted to come out from coming out, and those who were going in from going in. He attacked it on every side; every prince knew his part of the wall and every man was waiting in the place accorded him.

Piankhy received this grave news with hilarity. 'He heard these words with a great heart, and laughed wholeheartedly.' So it was that the informers sent His Majesty messengers from their cities every day, saying:

(*above*) A sphinx erected by Taharka, Piankhy's son and later successor.
(*opposite*) The feet of a pharaoh.
(*overleaf*) A painted coffret showing the weighing of a dead man's heart against the truth (represented by a feather), in the judgment of Osiris.

Wilt thou forget the land of the South and the nomes of the court of Nekhen? Tefnakhte is conquering them, and no one withstands him. Nemrat has laid low the walls of Nefrusy, where Kamose had done battle with the Hyksos, he himself has dismantled the fortifications, fearing that he might be taken and imprisoned in another city. And behold he is on his way to be the companion of his feet. He has sent back the water of His Majesty [those who were 'in a great man's water' were said to be his allies].

This time Piankhy considered that the moment for action had come. He ordered all the chiefs in Egypt to assemble troops, to harass the enemy, to capture people, livestock and ships, to keep the peasants from the fields and the labourers from their labour, and to prepare the siege of Hermopolis by fighting every day. And that is what they did.

Piankhy sent his troops two orders of the day. Here to begin with is the one about conduct to the enemy:

There must be no attack at night, but you must fight when you can be seen, according to the rules of the game. Announce the combat from a distance. If the enemy says that the soldiers or horsemen of some other city are late, then wait until his army has arrived. You will fight when he tells you to fight. If his allies find themselves elsewhere, you must wait for them. As for the princes he brings to help him, the Libyans, his faithful fighters: announce the combat to them by saying: 'You, whatever your name may be, you who command the troops, harness the best horses in your stable, take up your battle stations. You will learn that the god Amun sends us.'

Far from trying to take the enemy by surprise, Piankhy's soldiers had to leave him the time and means to assemble all his forces, even the forces which were far away. When he said he was ready, that was the moment to attack. God would give the better man the victory. This was the rule among the combatants who obeyed the orders of Amun, but the Aamu, who had no faith, did not announce their day of combat; they did their deed and vanished into their forests. (On the other hand, there are several examples in antiquity and the Middle Ages of combatants who suggested a day for the fight.)

The second order of the day concerns the conduct to be observed at Thebes:

When you reach the palace of Thebes opposite Ipet-Esut, you will enter the water and wash yourselves in the Nile, you will dress, and loosen your bow, and unbind your weapons. Do not boast that you are the masters of power, there is no power for those who work unknown to Amun. He keeps guard by the strength of his arms. A multitude will turn away from a small troop of men. A single man will capture a thousand. Sprinkle yourselves with the water of his altars. Kiss the earth before his face . . .

These two orders of the day spring from the same feeling, an absolute trust in the god who, alone, grants victory. 'They went down the river and came to Thebes, and acted according to His Majesty's words, and marched towards Ha-ninsu to announce the combat. Tefnakhte suffered a heavy defeat but succeeded in escaping. His Majesty's soldiers surrounded the city of the

Lievre [Hermopolis]; Nemrat had shut himself up inside, letting no one leave or enter it.' However, when Piankhy learned of what they had done, he became as furious as the panther. Did one have to leave them part of this army of the Delta? The victories at Oxyrhynchos, at Tench, and Castle of the Phoenix did not calm his rage. He went to Thebes to celebrate the great feast of Amun, and then took command of the army himself. Hermopolis, the city of the Lievre, continued to resist; Piankhy surrounded it with trenches and high walls, and his soldiers riddled the defenders with arrows and stones.

Eventually Hermopolis began to smell so badly that the citizens could no longer breathe. They prostrated themselves in supplication before the king. The messengers came and went with all sorts of presents. Even Nemrat's wife, Nesterit, prostrated herself in supplication to Piankhy's women, his daughters and sisters: 'We come to you so that you may appease the Horus, the all-powerful and triumphant master of the palace.' Nemrat himself brought a horse on the right and presented sistrums on the left. The king entered the palace and went into the temple of Thoth. The soldiers sang his praises. 'The women and the daughters of Nemrat praised him with women's wiles, but Piankhy did not turn his head towards them.' He went to the stables where the horses were kept, and when he saw that these noble animals had been allowed to starve, he cried:

As truly as I am alive, and love Re, and my nose flourishes in life, this is harder to my heart than all the harm you have done by your obstinacy. Do you not know that the shadow of the god is on me? I have not sinned against him. I was born of the divine womb. God ordained my existence from the egg. The divine seed is in me. I swear by his *ka* that I have not acted unknown to him, it is he who commands me to act.

Piankhy resumed his march towards the North. The King of Ha-ninsu (Heracleopolis) surrendered of his own accord. He had toyed with the idea of resistance but on the day of the fight he had found himself without friends and allies. All the fortified cities opened their gates, whatever their importance and whatever the size of their garrison. His Majesty warned them in these words: 'Behold, two paths lie before you. Choose which you prefer. Open the gates, and you will live. Shut them, and you will die. My Majesty does not pass a city when its gates are shut.' And then they opened them at once.

Piankhy was now in Lower Egypt. He warned the inhabitants of the nome of the White Wall.

Do not shut your gates. Do not fight. The first time I enter the palace of Chu, [victory?] will enter, when I leave she will leave. I suffer no impediment in my marches. I shall make an offering to Ptah and the gods of the White Wall [Memphis]. The White Wall will be safe and sound. Its children will not weep. Consider the nomes of the South. No one was slain there, except for the great traitors to the gods. No one was tortured, except for the rebels.

This engaging speech had no effect. During the night, the prince of Sais (Tefnakhte) reached the White Wall to deploy his soldiers and sailors, all the leaders of his army, the élite, eight thousand in number. The city was protected on the east by the high waters of the Nile, for it was still the season of the flood; everywhere else it was protected by high ramparts. Tefnakhte departed again as quickly as he had come, but he intended to return with a relief army.

Some of Piankhy's officers were in favour of a siege, and others were in favour of an assault; but His Majesty had built scaffoldings and ramps, and once again he grew angry like the panther. 'I live, I love Re, my father Amun favours me . . . I shall take all that as a waterspout.' Piankhy's soldiers took

A finely carved wooden vulture head with polychrome glass eyes.

possession of the enemy ships and the quay, and they stayed in the city. There
was a great massacre and a enormous haul of prisoners, but they took
measures to protect the temples. The city was purified with natron and resin.
The priests were put where they should be.

The capture of Memphis marked the end of military operations for
Piankhy. Now he was going to gather the fruits of his victory, and indulge his
predilection for ceremonies and rites. 'His Majesty went to Per . . . to make
his morning ablution. He performed the royal rites; entered the temple, made
a great oblation to his father Ptah at the South of his wall, oxen, sheep, fowl,
and all good things, and reached his dwelling.'

All the nomes in the territory of Memphis learned what had happened:

Pharaoh Taharka making offerings to the hawk, the most sacred bird.

The earth grew light and next day His Majesty went to the East to make a purification at Tum in Kher-Aha, to the Enneade of the gods in the temple of the Enneade which was there.

His Majesty went to Heliopolis by the mountain of Kher-Aha by the way of the god Sep at Kher-Aha.

His Majesty went to the tent which was west of the Ity canal. He purified himself. He washed himself in the lake of Qebehu. He washed his face in the primordial Nile where Re had washed his face. He went to the high dunes of Heliopolis to make an offering to the face of the god on his rising: a white cow, incense, resin and sweet-smelling plants. Then he went to the temple of Re, and entered the temple in adoration, like a chief master of ceremonies thanking God for driving back the king's enemies.

He purified with resin and libation. He presented flowers to the Castle of the Pyramidion.

He brought sustenance, he mounted the steps towards the great balcony, so that he might see Re in the Castle of the Pyramidion. The king himself went up, alone, he drew the bolts, opened the doors and saw his father Re in the Castle of the Pyramidion: the *mandjit* [the day barge] and the *mesketet* [the night barge] of Tum . . .

He brought back the two gates, set the clay, sealed it with the royal seal . . . None of the kings who were there entered after him. They prostrated themselves before His Majesty.

He entered the temple of Tum, and burned incense to his father Tumkhepri at Heliopolis.

King Osorkon came to see the beauty of His Majesty. The earth grew light and the next day His Majesty went to the quay, he went on board his ship, and he went to the quay of the Black Bull [a nome in the North]. His Majesty set up his tent to the south of To-Mehu, all the nobles who wore a feather, all the falconets, all the relations of the king of the West, of the East and of the isles of the middle came to see the beauty of His Majesty.

Prince Peteese invited King Piankhy to come to the Black Bull to see the god Khentamenty, and to enjoy the protection of the goddess Khut; everything he possessed was put at his disposal. 'In fact His Majesty collected the gold and the silver, the lapis and the turquoise, the linen and the furniture, the incense and the mares. The princes made an oath, except for one whose possessions were given to Peteese in recompense.' Tefnakhte in turn considered it futile to continue resistance. 'The fear of thee is in my body,' he wrote to his rival, 'and the terror of thee is in my bones. No longer do I sit in the beer-house, no longer do the harpists play for me.' He made peace proposals, and the king declared himself satisfied with them; the last of the cities which had not rallied to Piankhy also surrendered to him, and all the nomes of the South and North, of the West and East and Centre sent gifts to the places where His Majesty was.

The earth grew light, and men beheld the sovereigns of the South and North arrive to kiss the ground before His Majesty's Souls. And so the kings of the South and the princes of the North came to see the beauty of His Majesty. Their feet were like women's feet, but they did not enter the palace because they were uncircumcised, and because they ate fish, which was forbidden in the house of the king. Only Nemrat entered the king's palace, because he was pure and did not eat fish. All the others stood where they were, and none of them entered the house of the king.

Piankhy and his troops did not go beyond the nome of the Black Bull. All they thought of, now, was amassing their vast booty on board the ships: gold and silver, copper and raiment. They also took possession of ships from Syria, and from the land of the god (the land of Punt), which had anchored in the ports of the Delta, and left again for the South. The king's heart rejoiced. All the people came to the banks to acclaim him and to sing to his praises. Had he been very imprudent? Tefnakhte, his principal adversary, had withdrawn to Sais without any trouble. Other cities like Tanis and Sile had not even been threatened, and they might suddenly prove to be dangerous. Piankhy's departure for Upper Egypt really looks very much like an escape. Perhaps, after so many conquests, his soldiers had no great wish to fight again. These Africans were hardly excited by the conquest of the coast.

Back in his capital, in Napata, Piankhy had a magnificent stele engraved; and it is on this stele that he recounts his exploits with such wonderful complacency. In the centre he appears before Amun and Mut, together with his wives, and with King Nemrat, who is holding his horse with one hand and a sistrum with the other. It must be remembered that Nemrat was pure. Three other kings, eaters of fish, are kissing the ground: Osorkon, master of Bubastis and Re-nefer, a region near Tanis; Iuput, who had a domain in the very centre of the Delta; and the King of Ha-ninsu, Peftu-abast, who had a pretty gold statuette executed for his god Herichef.

The age of Piankhy is an age of very poor artistic activity. No building, in Napata or in Thebes, recalls his name. No sculptor, at least to our knowledge, has fixed the conqueror's features in sandstone or granite. His only monument is his stela, but that is enough to preserve his memory. In this brief study we have quoted texts which were dictated or inspired by a pharaoh. The stele of Napata, drawn up in a terse, direct style, is in the first rank of these texts.

We hardly need a statue in order to form an idea of Piankhy. The dominant feature of his character was piety; he did not compromise with the demands of his religion and he expected those around him to respect them too. The soldiers bathed in the Nile before they entered Thebes, and they respected the gods of the capital and all the gods whom they might encounter on the way. Piankhy refused to come into contact with the eaters of fish – many of whom were, moreover, uncircumcised. He liked horses, and his greatest reproach to Nemrat was that, in his stubbornness, he had caused suffering to those noble beasts. The wiles of women did not touch him. He asked his adversary to choose the day of the fight, and waited for him to be prepared.

He had no doubts about his divine origin. 'God has decreed my existence from the egg. The divine seed is in me. I swear by his *ka* that I do not act unknown to him. It is he who orders my deeds.' It seemed to him quite natural to plunder the vanquished: gold, silver, turquoise and lapis for him; food for his troops. In this, indeed, he conformed to custom. He was very generous to the gods, but it was the vanquished who had provided the sacrifices and offerings.

In composing the king of Napata's portrait, we have drawn the ideal portrait of a pharaoh. Piankhy's only failing was his failure to understand that no reign is truly great unless the arts have flourished.

Amasis, a Philhellene king

Until about the time of Piankhy, the great city of Sais, on the western side of the western Delta, had not played a very important part in politics. However, Tefnakhte, prince of the West, had allied a number of cities and nomes together against the Ethiopian aggressor. Piankhy overthrew this coalition, but, as we have seen, he could get no further than Athribis and he did not occupy Sais.

A little later, we find a Prince Neko at Sais. This prince considered the city as a family possession, and he handed it on to his son Psammetichus. With the help of Greek soldiers and sailors, he became sole master of Egypt, and began by driving out the Assyrians who had gained a footing there. One must consider him as the founder of dynasty XXVI, a dynasty which was to bring a long period of peace and prosperity to Egypt. This dynasty had a very strong tendency to return to the distant past, and to take their models from it, as if these ancient kings had known the secret of greatness.

Psammetichus's son, who was called Neko, like his grandfather, drew Egypt into a number of enterprises. He had acquired a fleet of triremes from the Corinthians, and he opened a canal which allowed people to reach the Red Sea by way of Bubastis and Pithom. This canal had in fact existed under the Ramses, and probably earlier, and the Saite kings only brought it back into use; but they did so in such a way that two triremes could go down it side by side.[1]

When the canal was opened to navigation, Neko sent off some vessels with Phoenician sailors – possibly they were Gibilites – on board; they had been ordered to come back to Egypt by way of the Mediterranean, as if people

(*opposite above*) Because hawks were venerated their embalmed bodies were often placed in tombs.

(*opposite below*) Figures of sacred animals: left, the cat sacred to the goddess Bastet; centre, the Apis bull; and right, the baboon sacred to Thoth.

(*above*) Head of a pharaoh of dynasty XXVI.

(*opposite*) The upper part of a grey granite statue of an unknown queen of the
Saite period in dynasty XXVI.

thought that Africa was some gigantic island. The voyage took three years, and a day came when the sun, which the sailors had had on their right, appeared on their left. They did not realise what they had done, but they had passed the Cape of Good Hope.[2]

Towards the end of Apries' reign, there occurred an event which cost the king his crown and shortened the life of the dynasty.[3] Egypt and Libya had long been united by a treaty of offensive and defensive alliance (Piankhy briefly alludes to it in his instructions to his army). Adicran, the Libyan king, was enraged by the presence of the Greeks at Cyrene, who were multiplying much too fast for his liking, and he summoned help from the Egyptians to get rid of the. Apries sent a great army – convinced that it would simply eat up the Greeks (Herodotus IV, 159). The encounter took place at Nasa on the Libyan

Twenty-sixth Dynasty relief of a procession.

coast. The Greeks were victorious, simply because their adversaries had had no experience of them. Very few returned to Egypt. Those who escaped safe and sound, and those who were friends of the dead, imagined that King Apries had sent them that far away to have them killed and to reign more easily over the rest of the population. Apries sent Amasis to them, who must have been some important functionary. He had been born at Siuph, a town near Sais. As his family was undistinguished, the Egyptians disdained him, but he earned their favour by his happy disposition, and showed them that a man cannot always be concerned with serious things. Far from being serious, he liked to drink and make merry and showed very little respect for other people's property. The unfortunate Apries was soon to find this out. While Amasis was speaking to the rebels, a man approached him, put a helmet on

his head and marked him out as king. Amasis accepted the honour. Apries, whose ruin had doubtless been decreed by the gods, sent someone called Patarbemis to the spot. Amasis, who happened to be on horseback, rose in his saddle and made an impolite noise. Patarbemis could obtain no other answer from him. Apries was furious, and, without pausing for reflection, he had his messenger's nose and ears cut off. The effect of this was disastrous, and all the Egyptians who supported Apries went over to Amasis, except for the mercenaries who marched to meet the Egyptians. The mercenaries fought, and were beaten, and Apries, who had thought himself invincible, was captured. Amasis, who was certainly not a bad man, assigned him Sais as his residence, where he already had his palace. Apries was well treated, but the Egyptians demanded his death. He was buried in the sepulchre of his fathers, near the sanctuary of Neith.

And there was Amasis sole master of Egypt. He gave himself a very simple titulary:

> Horus: He who establishes justice.
> Vulture-Cobra: Son of Neith, who governs the two lands.
> Golden Horus: Elect of the gods.
> King: Khnemibre [Khnum is the heart of Re].

He was careful not to have any quarrel whatever with the Greeks. He knew their worth; he was the most pro-Hellene of all his dynasty. Some people say that he married a daughter of Adiwan, king of Cyrene; others say that he married Ladice, the daughter of a private citizen. [4]

Their marriage was not very happy at first. Amasis could not consummate it, and husband and wife would burst into reproaches against each another. Ladice, fearing the wrath of Amasis, made a vow to Aphrodite: if the situation became normal the following night she would send her statue to Cyrene. Ladice fulfilled her vow, and the statue she sent to Cyrene still existed in the time of Herodotus. [4] As for Amasis, he gave offerings to Cyrene and to other parts of Greece: to Samos, because of his friendship for Polycrates; to Lindos, because the city was said to have been founded by the Danaides. Amasis had other Egyptian wives. The best-known, Tent-Khata, was the mother of the hereditary prince, Psammetichus III.

To finish with Amasis' enterprises abroad, we may recall that – according to Herodotus – he was the first pharaoh to occupy Cyprus. In fact the Egyptians knew the great island in the time of Thutmose III and Ramses II; on a clear day it could be seen from the Mediterranean coast, and they got copper from it. [5]

When a foreign ship had to unload its merchandise in an Egyptian port, it was only allowed to do so at Naucratis, a city west of Sais on the edge of the Anu canal. Amasis extended the privilege of the Greeks; he conceded all the surrounding country to them. But the Greeks are always inclined to take more than they are given, and they soon exceeded their limits. English scholars have found the traces of a great *temenos* and of less important *temene* in the ruins of Naucratis.[6] Amasis also gave the Greeks another proof of sympathy. He authorised them to make a collection to restore the temple of the Amphictyons at Delphi. The collection was fruitful and he increased it by a substantial personal gift.

The Saite period should have been a glorious period for Egyptian art. Artistic life had developed most markedly in the Delta, where the political centres, Sais, Memphis and Tanis, were found. In fact we have hardly any means of appreciating Saite buildings. But our museums are extremely rich in little bronzes of sacred animals, and one or two statues of individual people deserve to be praised. For round bosses and bas-reliefs the Saites simply took their models from the Old Kingdom; their work has no great originality, but it shows great skill.

Above all, they embellished their capital, Sais, the centre of the cult of Neith, their protecting goddess. The vast brick enclosure contains a sepulchre of Osiris as well as the temple of Neith. At Sais, in honour of Neith, Amasis built propylaea which are not only admirable as a whole but also because of their size and the quality of the stone that was used; he also consecrated colossi and sphinxes, either in limestone from Tura, or in granite from Aswan. He had a monolith, twenty-one cubits by fourteen by eight, transported to Sais; it was so heavy that they gave up the idea of installing it on the intended site and left it near the sanctuary. Naturally there were various stories to explain why it had been abandoned.[7]

Hardly anything remains of these buildings. A modern town, Sa el Hagar, was built on the ruins which kept it safe from the flood.[8] Champollion and Lepsius saw Sais better preserved than it is today. And, with the help of Herodotus, they were able to make a brief plan of it.

The enclosure is one of the most gigantic that we know. The larger side measures about seven hundred yards and the small one three hundred. The height of the wall may be gauged at forty-eight or fifty-one feet. The great temple already existed; Amasis added a pair of obelisks to it, propylaea superior to all the similar works which Herodotus knew. He added colossal statues, an avenue of sphinxes, and the tombs of the first Saite kings.[9]

For want of these works, we can point out a basalt sphinx found and preserved in Rome. It is easy to restore the defaced inscription: it belonged to King Khnemibre, son of the sun Ahmet (Amasis), son of Neith, who was loved by the great god Osiris in the Castle of the Wasp. The face has also been much damaged, and we shall discuss this later. The face is regular, even distinguished, but I do not know if it has preserved the features of Amasis for us. It might be called a model of sculpture. It was the same Amasis who raised a cenotaph to Osiris. There was a lake beside it, bordered with stone, recalling the circular lake at Delos, where there were nightly re-enactments of

(*overleaf left*) The mother goddess Isis. With her son Horus they became the popular deities of later Egypt and eventually the Queen of Heaven and the Holy Child.
(*overleaf right*) The lion-headed, destructive goddess, Sekhmet.

the sufferings Osiris had undergone.[10] At Memphis, Amasis also left works which deserve to be seen, such as the colossus lying in front of the temple of Ptah. A stela which was found at Tanis proves that Amasis had undertaken to build great walls of unburnt brick. It is engraved with marvellous care.[11]

The reign of Amasis was particularly happy for Egypt. The population grew steadily, thanks to the peace and to excellent administrative measures, which were the inspiration of Solon of Athens. But all things must come to an end. The reign of Amasis ended after forty-four years, and his mummy was laid in the tomb which he had prepared for himself in the great temple at Sais, opposite the tombs of the first Saite kings.

Amasis really left Egypt in a critical situation, exposed to the enterprises of a dangerous neighbour, Cambyses, king of the Persians.[12] Encouraged by his physician, who had a grudge against Amasis, Cambyses had asked him for his daughter. Amasis dared not refuse, and yet the marriage hardly pleased him; he knew quite well that Cambyses was only taking the princess as a concubine. He sent Princess Nitetis, Apries' daughter, to Persia with a rich dowry, and passed her off as his own child. But Nitetis did not leave Cambyses in error for long. 'O king, thou art the dupe of this man. I am in truth the daughter of Apries who was his master, against whom he rebelled with the Egyptians. I am the daughter of Apries, whom he has killed.' Cambyses burst into a great rage, but it is infinitely probable that the conquest of Egypt had already been decided.

These projects were greatly facilitated by the reports of a man of Halicarnassus, called Phanes, who also had a grudge against Amasis and knew Egypt well. Amasis thought himself well protected by the desert, which is terribly arid for a three-day march, but Cambyses negotiated with the king of the Arabs, who supplied the Persian army with water in leather bottles.

The two armies met at Pelusium, but Amasis was dead when the battle took place. It was an extremely violent battle. The Egyptians finally gave way and fled in disorder. That was the end of Egyptian grandeur. Cambyses went from Pelusium to the centre of the Delta.

When Memphis was captured, he made his way towards Sais. He entered the palace of Amasis, and gave orders for his mummy to be taken out of his tomb. He had it outraged in every conceivable way – according to Herodotus – and, finally, as the mummy could not be broken, he had it cast into a fire, just as a little later he had the statuettes of Ptah *pateque* cast into the flames. But was Herodotus well informed? Among the insults which had been inflicted on Amasis, he should certainly have mentioned the removal of the nose, for the nose has obviously been cut off the statue in Rome. A statue of Apries, preserved in Bologna, and a royal statue in Florence and another in Berlin have been even more seriously damaged, for the lips have been cut off as well as the nose. We might think that such barbaric treatment was only inflicted in exceptional cases in Egypt, but Haremhab's edict proves that the kings did not hesitate to punish very high dignitaries in this way. Amasis himself did not always spare his contemporaries.

While the other pharaohs whom we have portrayed were all born on the steps of the throne, Amasis was a man of the people; he owed his remarkable elevation to his good fortune as much as to his skill and his lack of scruples.

What remains of his long reign on the throne of Horus? The Egyptians recalled his gaiety (it could even verge on coarseness), and they were grateful to him for keeping peace, which is a guarantee of prosperity. If he had gathered artists round him – and Egypt has known so many of them – he would have been one of the greatest of the pharaohs.

Granite lid from the coffin of a dwarf.

Maps

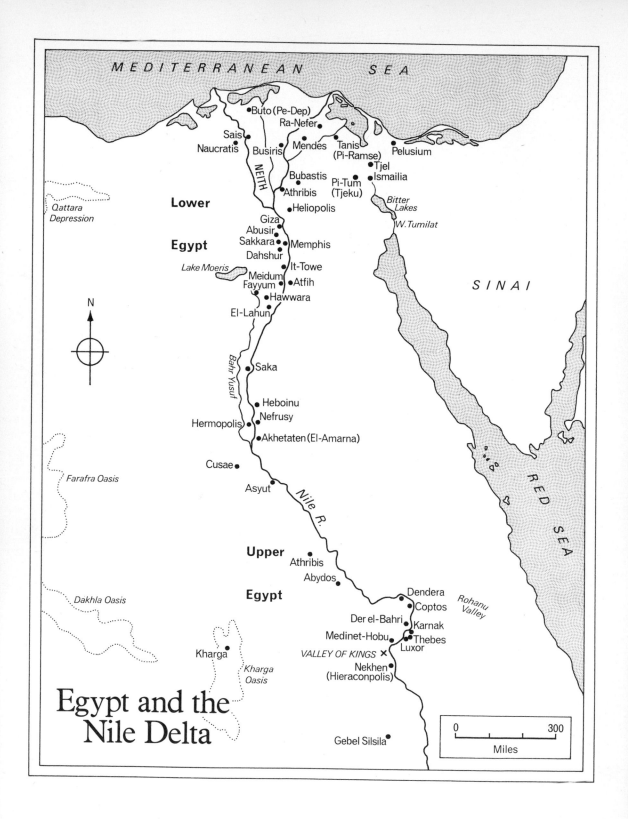

MEDITERRANEAN SEA

Buto (Pe-Dep)
Ra-Nefer
Sais
Naucratis
Busiris
Mendes
Tanis
(Pi-Ramse)
Pelusium
Tjel
Ismailia
NEITH
Bubastis
Pi-Tum
(Tjeku)
Athribis
Bitter
Lakes
Heliopolis
Lower
Qattara
Depression
W. Tumilat
Egypt
Giza
Abusir
Sakkara
Memphis
Dahshur
It-Towe
Lake Moeris
Meidum
Atfih
Fayyum
Hawwara
El-Lahun
SINAI
N
Bahr Yusuf
Saka
Heboinu
Nefrusy
Hermopolis
Akhetaten (El-Amarna)
Farafra Oasis
Cusae
Asyut
Nile R.
Upper
Athribis
Abydos
Egypt
Dendera
Rohanu
Valley
Coptos
Dakhla Oasis
Der el-Bahri
Karnak
Medinet-Hobu
Thebes
Kharga
Luxor
VALLEY OF KINGS ✕
Kharga
Oasis
Nekhen
(Hieraconpolis)
RED SEA

Egypt and the
Nile Delta

Gebel Silsila

0   300

Miles

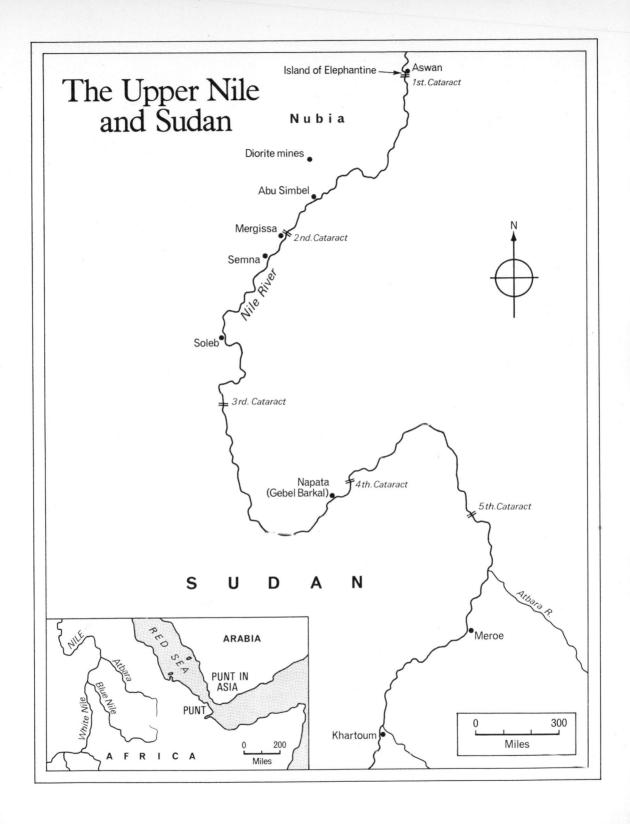

The Upper Nile and Sudan

N u b i a

Island of Elephantine → Aswan
1st. Cataract

Diorite mines

Abu Simbel

Mergissa
2nd. Cataract

Semna

Nile River

Soleb

3rd. Cataract

Napata
(Gebel Barkal)
4th. Cataract

5th. Cataract

S U D A N

Atbara R.

Meroe

N

Khartoum

0   300
Miles

ARABIA

RED SEA

NILE

Atbara

White Nile

Blue Nile

PUNT IN ASIA

PUNT

AFRICA

0   200
Miles

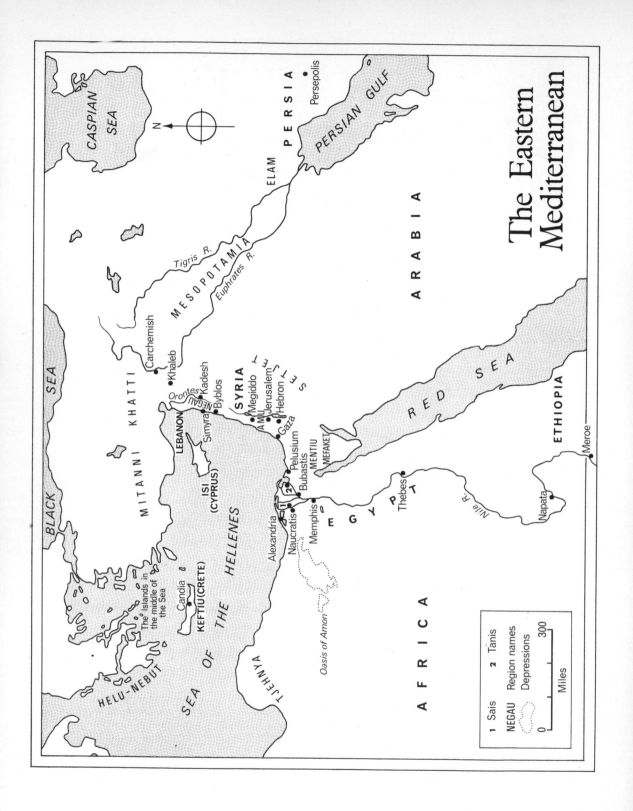

The Eastern Mediterranean

CASPIAN SEA

PERSIA

ELAM

Persepolis

PERSIAN GULF

N

Tigris R.

MESOPOTAMIA

Euphrates R.

ARABIA

BLACK SEA

Carchemish

Khaleb

MITANNI KHATTI

Kadesh

Orontes

NEGAU

Byblos

Simyra

LEBANON

SYRIA

Megiddo

AMU

Jerusalem

Hebron

Gaza

SETJET

Pelusium

Bubastis

MENTIU

MEFAKET

RED SEA

ETHIOPIA

Meroe

ISI (CYPRUS)

Alexandria

Naucratis

1 2

Memphis

EGYPT

Thebes

Nile R.

Napata

SEA OF THE HELLENES

The Islands in the middle of the Sea

Candia

KEFTIU (CRETE)

HELU-NEBUT

TSEHENYA

Oasis of Amon

AFRICA

1 Sais   2 Tanis

NEGAU Region names

Depressions

0   300

Miles

270

Chronological list of pharaohs mentioned

conjectural dates BC ARCHAIC

Dynasties I and II

OLD KINGDOM

Dynasty III

c.2620 **Dynasty IV**
Snofru
Cheops
Dedefre
Chephren
Mycerinus

c.2480 **Dynasty V**
Unis (the last king)

c.2340 **Dynasty VI**
Teti I
Pepi I
Meryre
Pepi II

Djoser

Cheops

Amenemnes III

FIRST INTERMEDIATE

Dynasties VII and VIII

Dynasties IX and X

MIDDLE KINGDOM

Dynasty XI

C.2212   **Dynasty XII**

Amenemnes I
Sesostris I
Amenemnes II
Sesostris II
Sesostris III
Amenemnes III
Sebeknofru

SECOND INTERMEDIATE

Dynasties XIII–XVII (including the Hyksos)

Sesostris I

Queen Hatshepsut

Thutmose III

NEW KINGDOM

Dynasty XVIII

1575–1550	Ahmose
1550–1528	Amenhotep I
1528–1510	Thutmose I
1510–1490	Thutmose II
1490–1468	Hatshepsut
1490–1436	Thutmose III
1436–1413	Amenhotep II
1413–1405	Thutmose IV
1405–1367	Amenhotep III
1367–1350	Amenhotep IV (Akhenaten)
1350–1347	Smenkhare
1347–1339	Tutankhamun
1339–1335	Ay
1335–1308	Haremhab

Dynasty XIX

1308	Ramses I
1309–1291	Seti I
1290–1224	Ramses II
1224–1214	Merenptah
	Amenemses
1208–1202	Siptah
	Seti II
	Interim anarchy, ending with a Syrian usurper called Arsu

Amenhotep III

Akhenaten

Tutankhamun

Dynasty XX

1184–1182 Setnakhte
1182–1151 Ramses III
1151–1145 Ramses IV
            Ramses V–XII

LATE NEW KINGDOM

c. 1087–945 **Dynasty XXI**

           Including:
           Smendes
c.1055   Psusennes

c.945–730 **Dynasty XXII** (Libyans)

c.950   Sheshonk I
           Osorkon I
           Takelot I
           Osorkon II
           Sheshonk II
           Takelot II
           Sheshonk III
           Pemu
           Sheshonk IV

Ramses II

Merenptah

Psusennes

c.817?–730	**Dynasty XXIII** (Libyans)
c.720–715	**Dynasty XXIV** (Ethiopians)
	Dynasty XXV (Ethiopians)
	Including:
751–730	Piankhy

SAITE

Dynasty XXVI

664–610	Psammetichus I
610–595	Neko
595–589	Psammeticus II
589–570	Apries
570–526	Amasis
526–525	Psammetichus III

LATE

Dynasties XXVII–XXXI

Queen Karoma

Taharka

Pharaoh of Dynasty XXVI

Notes

p. 13 **Snofru**

1 Pap. Prisse, p. 2, *Sagesse de Kegemni*.
2 *Annales du Service des Ant. d'Egypte*, LI, 577 & sqq.
3 *Annales de l'Ancien Empire*, Sethe, *Urkunden*, I, 236.
4 Lepsius, *Denkmäler*, II, 2a.
5 G. A. Reisner, *The Tomb of Aetep-heres, the mother of Cheops*.
6 Papyrus Westcar, tr. fr. Lefebvre, *Romans et Contes égyptiens*, 77.
7 *Conte prophétique*, tr. fr. ibid., 96.
8 See: Al. Varille, *A propos des pyramides de Snefrou*, Cairo, 1947.

p. 21 **Cheops**

1 Et. Drioton, *Une liste de rois de la IVe dynastie dans l'Ouadi Hammamat*, Bulletin de la société française d'égyptologie, no. 17 (1954).
2 R. Engelbach, *The quarries of the western Nubian desert and the ancient road to Tueskha*, Anna. du Serv. XXXVIII, 369 & sqq.
3 W. S. Smith, *Sculpture and painting in the Old Kingdom*, Boston, 1946, pl. 39 & p. 157.
4 See: Maspero, *Contes populaires*, Introduction, p. XXIII.

p. 36 **Pepi II**

1 Sethe, *Urkunden*, I, 128.
2 P. Montet, *Drame d'Avaris*, 26.
3 Sethe, *Urkunden*, I, 280 & sqq.
4 G. Posener, *Le Conte de Neferkare et du Général Sitene*, Rev. d'Egypte. XI, 119.
5 G. Jéquier, *Le Monument funéraire de Pepi II*, 3 vol. Cairo, 1936.

p. 50 **Amenemnes I**

1 On Qem-Ur, see G. Posener, *Littérature et politique dans l'Egypte de la XIIème dynastie*, 25.
2 On the Prince's Wall, see G. Posener, op. cit., 25–6.
3 Ibid., 30 and all chapter I.
4 Quoted by A. H. Gardiner, *Egypt of the Pharaohs*, p. 439, No. 2.
5 Kêmi, XIII, 97.
6 Gauthier & Jequier, *Fouilles de Licht*, 87–107.

p. 56 **Amenemnes III**

1 Sethe, *Die Achtung feindlicher Fürsten Völken und Dinge auf altägyftichen Ton Gesässcherben des M. R.*, Berlin 1926.
2 Lepsius, *Denkmäler*, II, 136.
3 Montet, *Byblos et l'Egypte*, no. 610.
4 Porter and Moss, *Topography and bibliography*, IV, 98–101.
5 Porter and Moss, ibid., IV, 77–8.
6 Porter and Moss, ibid., IV, 100.

p. 68 **Kamose**

1 Josephus, *Against Apion*, I, 75.
2 Pap. Sallier I, Brit. Mus. 10 185 the beginning, cf. J. E. A., vol. 36.
3 A. H. Gardiner, *The defeat of the Hyksos by Kamose*, Carnarvon Tablet I, J.E.A., III, 95.
4 P. Lacau, *Une stèle du roi Kamose*, in Ann. du Serv. XXXIX, 245.
5 Labib Habachi, *Preliminary report on Kamose steles and the inscribed blocks found in the foundations of two statues at Karnak* in Ann. du Serv, LIII, with a quite good plate. I am indebted to M. L. Habachi for a good impression which only leaves a few groups uncertain.
6 Porter and Moss, *Topographical bibliography*, I, 36.

p. 80 **Queen Hatshepsut**

1 Vandier, *Manuel d'archéologie égypt.*, III, 300–301.
2 Naville, *The temple of Deir el Bahari*, 6 vol.
3 C. Desroches-Noblecourt, *Deux grands obélisques précieux d'un sanctuaire à Karnak*, Rev. d'Egypt., VIII, 47.
4 P. Montet, *Eternal Egypt*, 245.
5 Naville, op. cit., III, pl. 69 & sqq.

p. 95 **Thutmose III**

1 For the campaigns of Thutmose III one must refer to the annals of this king at Karnak (Sethe, *Urkunden*, IV, 647 sqq.) and to the stele of Napata published by G. A. Reisner and M. B. Reisner, *Zeitschrift für aeg. spr.* 49, 1939, 24–39.
2 Sethe, *Urkunden*, IV, 890 sqq.
3 Sethe, ibid., 707; Kêmi, XIII, 67 sqq.
4 Porter and Moss top. bibl. II, 27 sqq.
5 Wreszinski, Atlas, II, 26–31.
6 Sethe, *Urkunden*, IV, 614.
7 Sethe, *Urkunden*, IV, 1094 sqq.
8 Cairo 38574.
9 Painted picture in the king's tomb. V. Loret, Bull. de l'Inst. eg. 1898, pl. 6.
10 Varille B. I. F. A. O. XLI, 31 sqq. (portrait de Senmout, Winlock, Exc. at Deir el Bahari N. Y. 1942, pl. 63).
11 Sethe, *Urkunden*, IV, 895.

p. 117 **Amenhotep III**

1 Lefebvre, *Sur l'obélisque du Latran*, Mélanges Picard II, p. 586 93.
2 *Urkunden*, IV, p. 1740.
3 Thureau-Dangin, *Nouvelles lettres d'Amarna*, Rev. d'Assyriologie, p. 91 sqq.
4 *Urkunden*, IV, p. 1738.
5 Thureau (Dangin, op. cit.).
6 *Urkunden*, IV, p. 1741.
7 Varille & Robichon, *Le temple du scribe royal Amenhotep, fils de Hapou*.
8 Kemi, XV, 1959, p. 23–32.
9 Varille, Bull. de l'Institut français du Caire, XLI, 1942, p. 25–30.

p. 134 **Amenhotep IV**

1 Sandman, *Texts from the Time of Akhenaton* (Bibliotheca Aegyptica VIII, Bruxelles, 1938, p. 112 & sqq.)
2 Id., p. 120 & sqq.
3 Id., p. 36–7.

p. 146 **Tutankhamun**

1 On Tutankhamun's tomb, Carter and Mace, *The Tomb of Tut-Ankh-Amen*, London, 1923–33; Chr. Desroches-Noblecourt, *Vie et Mort d'un Pharaon*, Paris, 1963.
2 Cairo 38 488.
3 Bennet, Journal of Egyptian Archaeology, XXV, 1939, p. 8–15.
4 Benedite, Monuments Piot, Paris 1920, p. 47–68.
5 Davies & Gardiner, *The Tomb of Huy viceroy of Nubia in the reign of Tut-Ankh-Amen*, pl. XIX–XX.
6 Wolf, *Das Schöne Fest von Opet*, Leipzig, 1931.

p. 164 **Ramses the Great**

1   P. Montet, Comptes rendus de l'Académie des Inscriptions de Belles Lettres, 1937, p. 418–26.
2   S. Sauneron, Bull. de la Soc. Hist. et Geogr. de l'Isthme de Suez, V, 1954, p. 54–8.
3   Kemi XIII, 1939, p. 54–5.
4   Gauthier, *La grande inscription dédicatoire d'Abydos* (Bibliothèque d'Etudes IV), Le Caire, 1912.
5   Cerny, Journal of Egyptian Archaeology XXXII, 1946, 24–30.
6   Gauthier, op. cit.
7   Gauthier, op. cit.
8   Sethe, *Zeitschrift für Aegyptische Sprache*, 1907, p. 30.
9   Pap. Anastasi III, I, II to 3, 9.
10 Editions des documents, Ch. Kuent *La bataille de Qadesh*, Cairo, 1928–34. Translation A. H. Gardiner, *The Kadesh inscriptions of Ramses II*, Oxford, 1960.
11 Langdon & Gardiner, Journal of Egyptian Archaeology, VI, 1920; p. 173–205.
12 Pap. Anastasi II, I, I to 2, 5.
13 Ch. Kuentz, Annales du Service des Antiquités XXV, 1925, p. 181–238.
14 Tresson, *La stèle de Kouban* (Bibliothèque d'Étude IX), Cairo, 1922.

p. 197 **Merenptah**

1   Grand texte de Karnak, Max Müller, *Egyptological Researches*, I, pl. 17–32.
2   Stèles, Le Caire, Catalogue général 34 025, V° L. 26–8 édition Lacau.

p. 204 **Ramses III**

1   Philadelphie 13727, Caire 12149.
2   Medinet-Habou, p. 109–10.
3   Id. pl. 29.
4   Id. pl. 75.
5   Harris Papyrus, 77, 1–5.
6   Medinet-Habou, pl. 32.
7   Medinet-Habou, pl. 37.
8   Harris Papyrus, 78, 9–12.
9   Medinet Habou, pl. 35.
10 Id. pl. 117.
11 Loret, *La résine de térébinthe chez les anciens Egyptiens*.
12 Harris Papyrus, 77, 9678, I.
13 Gardiner, *Journal of Egyptian Archaeology*, V. 1918, p. 132–3.
14 Edition du Papyrus Harris par Erichsen, dans Bibliotheca Aegyptia, V, 933.
15 De Buck, *Journal of Egyptian Archaeology*, XXIII, 1937, p. 152–64.

p.221 **Psusennes**

1   Le Drame d'Avaris, Paris, 1941.
2   For all the facts and documents in this chapter: Mission Montet: *Les Constructions et le tombeau de Psousennes à Tanis*, Paris, 1951.

p. 232 **Sheshonk I**

1   Harris Papyrus, 77, 5–7.
2   *Le Drame d'Avaris*, p. 197–8.
3   Reliefs and inscriptions at Karnak III, 1954.
4   *Byblos et l'Egypte*, p. 54–7.
5   Caminos, Journal of Egyptian Archaeology, XXXVIII, 1951, 46–9.
6   Mission Montet: *Les Constructions et le tombeau de Psousennes*, no. 226–7.
7   P. Montet excavated extensively at Tanis (among other Egyptian sites).

p. 243 **Piankhy**

1   Edition de la Stèle de Piankhy, *Urkunden*, III, p. 1–56.
2   Mélanges Maspero, I, fasc. 4, 1961, p. 151–9.

p. 254 **Amasis**

1   Herodotus, II, 158.
2   Id., II, 159.
3   On this event: Herodotus, II, 162 and 169.
4   Herodotus, II, 181.
5   Id., II, 182.
6   Id., II, 178.
7   Id., II, 175–6.
8   Labib Habachi, *Ann. du Serv. des Antiquités*, XLII, 1942, p. 396–416.
9   Porter and Moss, *Topographical Bibliography VII*, p. 416.
10   Herodotus, II, 171.
11   Kêmi, VIII, 1946, p. 40–43, pl. IV–V.
12   Herodotus, III, 1–16.

Index

Meryetre, Queen, 110
Meryre, 38, 49
Mesedsure, 218
Mesher, the, 206, 207
Meshwesh, the, 206, 234
mesketet, 29, 252, 321
Mesopotamia, 24, 223
Meten, 16
Middle Kingdom, the, 20, 24, 32, 49, 62, 66, 84, 96, 99, 114, 127, 128
Min, 42, 43, 44, 50, 120, 211
Min-Nekt, 82
Minoan art, 142
Minya, 244
Misphragamuthosis, 95
Mitanni, 99, 101, 117, 120, 131, 133, 138
Moeris, 59
Moeris, Lake, 64, 66, 67
Moiris, 59
Monthu, 50, 98, 113, 117, 177, 180
mortuary temple, 13, 15, 16, 19, 20, 22, 24, 64, 110, 114, 121, 153, 154, 200
Moses, 198, 200, 203
Muqed, 210
Mut, 127, 152, 235, 253
Mutemuia, Queen, 117, 128
Mutesallim, 236
Mutnodjme, 223, 231
Mutnofre, 81
Mycerinus, 15, 22, 36

Nahrin, 96, 119
Napalte, 223
Napata, 146, 243, 253, 254
Nasa, 258
Naucratis, 260, 261
Nebet, 215
Nebetu, Queen, 110
Nebkchepeshre, 70
Nebnechi, 234
Nebnenef, 170
Neferkare Amenemsut, 224
Neferiru, 110
Neferti, 53
Nefertiti, Queen, 134, 138, 139, 141, 143, 144, 146
Nefertum, 215
Nefrure, 84
Nefrusy, 74, 79, 248
Nega, 82
Nega Khasut, 68
Negau, 14, 86, 99
Negroes, 167
Neit, 221
Neith, Queen, 38
Neith, 260, 261
Nekhen, 49, 151, 248
Nekhen, nome of, 151
Neko, 254

Nemrat, 234, 248, 249, 253
Nesterit, 249
Neter, 243
Netjrikhe, 12
New Kingdom, the, 14, 29
Nile, River, 12, 24, 29, 41, 42, 53, 62, 64, 86, 106, 110, 114, 124, 128, 131, 134, 141, 151, 168, 170, 184, 188, 197, 198, 200, 211, 212, 244, 248, 252, 253
Ni-Maat-Hep, 16
Nimmuaria, 117, 131
Nine Arches, the, 215
Ninlil, 223
Nitetis, 264
Nitocris, Queen, 81
Niy, 99
Nofretari, Queen, 110, 181
nome, 14, 16, 21, 36, 44, 52, 62, 64, 66, 70, 79, 120, 138, 151, 170, 197, 211, 243, 249, 251, 252
Nubia, 24, 55, 59, 77, 79, 101, 138, 141, 144, 166, 200, 208, 232, 242, 243
Nufrit, 16
Nut, 110, 231

obelisks, 82, 84, 90, 100, 117, 127, 138, 194, 261
Old Kingdom, the, 14, 24, 29, 49, 53, 55, 62, 81, 114, 261
Onkhefenmut, 229, 231
Onnofris, 168
Onuris, 170
Opet, feast of, 152
Orontes, River, 99, 171, 177, 179
Oryx, nome of the, 14, 21
Osiris, 35, 55, 120, 141, 164, 166, 168, 170, 185, 211, 214, 215, 218, 261, 264
Osorkon, 252, 253
Osorkon I, 234, 242
Osorkon II, 242
Oxen region, 232
Oxyrhynchos, 249

Paihuti, 234
palace, 14, 21, 44, 55, 64, 128, 139, 140, 141, 151, 170, 181, 194, 210, 211, 212, 225
Palermo Stone, the, 14
Palestine, 56, 96, 198, 200, 235, 236, 239, 243
Parotiu, 87
Patarbemis, 260
Payonkh, 243
Payt, 212
Pe, 124
Peftu-abast, 253
pehu, 62, 66
Peleset, the, 208, 211
Pelusium, 53, 96, 171, 264

Pentawere, 215
Pepi I, 21, 38, 49
Pepi II, 36, 38, 41, 42, 43, 44, 49, 56, 164
Per-Nu, 14
Persepolis, 120
Persia, 264
Peru-nefer, 86
Per-Ur, 14
Peteese, 252
Phanes, 264
Philistines, the, 206
Phoenicia, 86, 172, 236, 254
Piabekkamen, 218
Piankhy, 243, 244, 248, 249, 250, 251, 252, 254, 258
Pi-Hariroth, 200
Pi-Hathor, 77
Pinudjem, 167, 224
Pi-Ramesse, 171, 179, 180, 188, 194, 197, 198, 200, 203, 210, 211, 215, 223, 229
Pithom, 254
Pi-Tum, 171, 200, 235
Pi-yer, 198
Pleader of Memphis, the, 44
Polychrates, 260
Prince's Wall, the, 53, 54, 59
Prisse d'Avesne, 100
Psammetichus, 254
Psammetichus III, 260
Psusennes, 221, 223, 224, 225, 228, 229, 231, 234, 235, 242
Ptah, 14, 22, 44, 52, 141, 150, 151, 152, 171, 172, 177, 179, 198, 210, 215, 249, 251, 264
Ptah-hotep, 36
Ptah-mose, 150
Puadjit, 180
Punt, 38, 41, 42, 44, 84, 90, 100, 106, 127, 210, 253
Puntiu, the, 90, 106
pyramid, 14, 16, 19, 20, 21, 32, 35, 36, 38, 44, 49, 55, 56, 64, 66, 67, 114
  Great Pyramid, 21, 29, 35
  Rhomboidal Pyramid, 15, 19
  Step Pyramid, 20

Qebehu, 252
Qem-Ur, 53

Ra-henit, 66
Rahotep, 16
Ramesseum, the, 128, 172, 185, 188
Rampsinite, 221
Ramses I, 164, 204
Ramses II, 12, 54, 127, 164, 166, 168, 170, 171, 172, 177, 178, 179, 180, 181, 184, 185, 188, 194, 197, 204, 206, 207, 210, 218, 221, 225, 231, 236, 239, 254, 260

Ramses III, 12, 200, 204, 206, 207, 208, 211, 214, 215, 218, 221, 225, 232, 234
Ramses IV, 221
Ramses VI, 163
Ramses IX, 114, 221, 223, 229, 243
Ra-nefer, 253
Re, 14, 36, 90, 98, 141, 153, 168, 170, 171, 172, 177, 179, 181, 185, 204, 234, 239, 249, 250, 252
Red Sea, the, 22, 42, 44, 64, 84, 86, 171, 254
Rehoboam, 235, 236
Reisner, 16, 99, 243
Rekhmire, 106
Retjnu, the, 54, 77, 96, 100, 106, 151
Rib-Addi, 119, 151
Roads of Horus, 53
Rohanu, 22, 24, 50, 64
Romans, the, 128, 208
Rosetta, River, 207

Sa el Hagar, 261
Sahure, 44, 86
Sais, 232, 250, 253, 254, 259, 260, 261, 264
Saite kings, 24
Saka, 79
Sakhebu, 36
Sakkara, 20, 36
Satire of Professions, the, 55
Satis, 127
Satyah, Queen, 110
Schaeffer, M. Cl., 154
Sea of Rushes, 200
sea peoples, the, 208, 211, 218
Seaports of Incense, 41
Seaports of Pine, 41
Sebeknofrure, Queen, 67, 81
Sed festival, 211
Segub, 224
sehent, 44
Sekenenre, 70
Sekhemkhet, 12, 15
Sekhet, 215
Sekhmet, 127, 215
Sem, 168
Semna (place), 59
Semna (person), 82
Semnen, 84
Senemut, 84, 90, 95, 96, 106
Sep, 252
serdab, 12, 49
Service des Antiquités, the, 29, 44, 168
Sesehat, 90
Sesostris I, 53, 54, 55, 56, 127
Sesostris II, 56
Sesostris III, 53, 56, 59, 68, 95, 110, 121

Set, 52, 70, 153, 164, 166, 171, 177, 179, 180, 204, 215, 221, 223, 224
Sethe, 44
Seti I, 150, 164, 166, 168, 170, 171, 204, 206, 239
Seti II, 200
Sheklesh, the, 197, 208, 211
Sherden, the, 179, 197, 206, 208, 211, 232
Sheshonk I, 231, 232, 234, 235, 236, 239, 242
Sheshonk II, 235, 242
Sheshonk III, 235, 242
ships and shipbuilding, 14, 15, 22, 24, 41, 42, 77, 84, 86, 87, 99, 101, 106, 152, 153, 188, 208, 210, 248, 250, 251, 253, 254, 260
Shosu, the, 177
Shuttarna, 119
Sile, 253
silver, 77, 98, 181, 254
Simyra, 99, 172
Sinai, 12, 15, 22, 24, 82, 110, 120
Sinuhe, 53, 54, 55
Sisine, 44
Sitamun, 120, 149
Siuph, 259
Smendes, 223
Smenkhare, 146
Snofru, 12, 13, 14, 15, 16, 18, 19, 20, 21, 22, 24, 53, 82, 110
solar boats, 29, 32, 117
solar temples, 36
Soleb, 120, 121, 146
Solomon, 70, 235, 236
Soped, nome of, 53, 197, 215
Sopek, 64, 67
Sphinx, the, 21, 32, 35
sphinxes, 90, 117, 128, 235, 261
state ships, 15, 32, 82, 127, 168, 210, 214
Stele of Israel, 198, 200
Strabo, 64
Sukkiims, the, 236
Suppiluliumas, 163
Susa, 234
Susinak, 234
Sutekh, 179, 181
Suti, 121
Syria, 14, 42, 53, 56, 77, 96, 99, 100, 103, 139, 141, 144, 151, 153, 166, 172, 180, 204, 206, 208, 211, 218, 223, 232

Taanach, 96, 98
Tadukhipa, 120, 138
Tahpenes, 235
Takelot, 234
Takelot II, 242
Tanis, 22, 70, 184, 221, 223, 224,

225, 228, 235, 242, 253, 261, 264
Teaching of Amenemnes in Fifteen Verses, the, 55
Tefnakhte, 243, 248, 250, 253, 254
Tench, 249
Tent-Khata, 260
Tentsepeh, 234
Terraces of Incense, 84; *see also* Punt
Terraces of Turquoise, 22
Teti, 29, 36, 38, 41, 56, 74
Teudjoi, 244
Thebes, 50, 70, 77, 82, 90, 96, 99, 100, 110, 113, 114, 115, 117, 118, 121, 124, 128, 134, 138, 146, 149, 150, 153, 164, 168, 170, 171, 172, 177, 185, 188, 198, 200, 221, 224, 225, 239, 243, 248, 249, 253
Thoth, 35, 90, 117, 141, 215, 225, 249
Thueris, 154
Thutmose, sculptor, 146, 151
Thutmose I, 81, 117
Thutmose II, 81, 95, 110
Thutmose III, 12, 29, 92, 95, 98, 99, 100, 102, 103, 110, 113, 114, 115, 117, 138, 144, 153, 154, 167, 172, 210, 243, 260
Thutmose IV, 117, 138, 153
Thuty, 82
timber, 14, 15, 77, 82, 86, 90, 99, 119, 151, 210
titulary, royal, 13, 21, 36, 50, 59, 80, 81, 95, 117, 134, 139, 164, 166, 167, 204, 206, 223, 234, 235, 260
Tiye, Queen, 117, 120, 127, 128, 133, 134, 143
Tiye Merenese, Queen, 204
Tjehnyu, the, 15, 54, 56, 101, 197, 198, 206, 234
Tjekker, 208
Tjeku, the, 200
Tjemeh, the, 54, 56, 197
Tjey, 36
Tjikarbaal, 223
Tjuia, 120, 149
To-Chemua, 243
tomb, 12, 14, 16, 19, 22, 29, 80, 84, 110, 121, 144, 149, 153, 154, 163, 167, 168, 197, 200, 218, 221, 223, 225, 228, 264
tomb of the Harpist, 218
To-Mehu, 252
To-neter, 210
triremes, 254
Troglodytes, 101
Tuia, Queen, 166
Tum, 153, 212, 214, 239, 252
Tunip, 99, 171